AF730756

Thrive

A guide for new lawyers

By Elizabeth Fairon

First published 2024 by Elf Law Pty Ltd, Australia

Produced by Independent Ink

Cover design by EM
Typeset in Bembo MT Pro by Post Pre-press Group, Brisbane

ISBN 978-0-6486371-9-6 (paperback)
ISBN 978-0-6486371-7-2 (kindle)

Never underestimate your power to thrive.

Contents

Introduction

Do you remember the first time the glimmering thought of becoming a lawyer crossed your mind? It was likely a moment woven with personal dreams, aspirations, and emotional ambitions. Perhaps you meticulously pondered the type of lawyer you aspired to be, imagining yourself standing tall in courtrooms, negotiating pivotal deals, or crafting meticulous legal strategies. Or, perhaps your path to the legal world was less defined, and you "fell into it" following a path of curiosity – just like I did. Regardless of the journeys we embarked upon, we all share a common thread: we chose to dive into the captivating world of law, and that, my friend, marks you as the future of the legal profession.

If the mere thought of this profound responsibility sends a shiver down your spine, consider yourself on the right track to thriving as a lawyer. Many law students and fresh legal minds often find themselves grappling with a formidable chasm – the gap between the theoretical prowess they acquire in classrooms and the pragmatic wisdom required to navigate what can be a convoluted practice of law. It's a divide that, more often than not, goes unaddressed. As a result, young lawyers, brimming with enthusiasm but lacking practical knowledge, find themselves wrestling with the intricate dance of demanding clients, towering workloads, and thorny ethical quandaries.

These challenges can become more than just roadblocks; they can morph into chronic stress, anxiety, and even depression. I've witnessed the toll it takes on bright legal minds, pushing some into the clutches of severe health issues. Tragically, many have left the law and turned away from the profession they once aspired to join. It's a narrative that should never be accepted as the norm, and it's a narrative I'm determined to reshape.

Two of the most significant issues facing our profession are the prevalence of mental health issues and burnout among lawyers. Left unchecked, these two factors can drastically impact how we practice law.

Mental health issues are a significant factor in the legal profession. When things go wrong in your career, the possibility of suffering from mental health issues increases.

The findings of two studies conducted in 2016, published by the American Bar Association in 2017, revealed the extent to which issues such as substance use and abuse, suicidal thoughts, depression, and anxiety were prevalent among law students and young lawyers. The study involved 3,300 law students from 15 schools and 13,000 working lawyers.

American Bar (2017) found that 25% of the students were on the verge of alcoholism while 17% reported feeling depressed, 37% said they had mild to severe anxiety, and 6% had experienced suicidal thoughts in the previous year alone.

Of the working lawyers surveyed, 11.4% had suicidal thoughts, 19% suffered from severe anxiety, and 28% suffered from depression.

Unfortunately, there's more.

According to a John Hopkins University study in 1990, lawyers were 3.6 times more prone to depression than workers from other professions, with drug abuse rates at 3.6% and alcohol abuse at 20.6%. Whilst that study dates to 1990, the findings are still relevant today with ongoing alarming statistics.

The Law Society of South Australia counts a career in law as one of the two professions with the highest prevalence of mental illness (Neaverson, 2021).

Neaverson (2021) states that the very traits that define lawyers, such as their unwavering work ethics, meticulous attention to detail, and perfectionism, also predispose them to stress, anxiety, and depression.

In Britain, 1 in 15 junior lawyers had suicidal thoughts, and 93.5% of the 1800 respondents experienced stress in their occupation (Walters, 2019). Despite such findings, mental health continues to be a taboo subject.

As the American Bar (2017) states, law students are afraid of others finding out they have mental health issues because they fear they will not be admitted to the bar or get a job if others find out they have a problem. Similar results came out of the South Australian Law Society Study, with participants there indicating they would be unlikely to seek help or talk about the issue – firstly because they thought that they would not be believed and secondly because they had no confidence in the process or discussion – either the procedure itself or the confidentiality of that process.

So, instead of seeking help, they suffer in silence.

The second major factor is **burnout**.

"I don't want to be a lawyer anymore."

In 2016, I said those words. And I meant it.

Burnout isn't a new topic, but it comes up regularly, particularly in the practice of law, and it's something that we need to talk about, recognise, and manage.

When I'm on my way into burnout, I notice that I am more tired than usual, stuck, just going through the motions. I think the answers to questions like "How are you going?" get more and more honest the closer you get to burnout. "I'm great," "busy," to "good," "Actually, I'm pretty tired," to "pretty exhausted." Interestingly, we rarely say, "I'm not okay" – I'm getting better at that, though.

Every day, work seems more and more relentless. The ability to send an email and demand an urgent response is real. Everything seems urgent, and we've adapted to respond that way – we have allowed it to happen. Long gone are the days of letters sent and received in the mail to set the pace of how matters are managed, so we keep going along reasonably fast, constantly 'on', waiting for the next thing.

My burnout journey came from a combination of those things – that pace, doing too much, not stopping, no breaks and exhaustion. It was only on reflection that I realised what I experienced was burnout.

My legal career started in 2005. I worked hard. I wanted to impress my boss, and I learned quickly that my billable hours and monthly budget directly related to my ability to earn more money. I would do the figures every six to twelve months, work out my annual target, and ask for a raise. Kept working.

In 2009, I was offered partnership to recognise my contribution to our firm.

I kept working and billing. I transitioned from an employee with annual leave entitlements to a self-employed owner. I rarely took holidays; when I did, they were limited, and I would still check in with the team. In early 2015, I bought my senior partner out of our partnership. I'd just ticked over my 10th year for those doing the maths.

Now, I was a business owner in my own right. It was all on me. I set about making necessary changes, bringing in new people, fixing the culture, and working with limited holidays. In 2016, I completed a leadership program and signed up for a 40-week business accelerator program. I kept going, pushing myself to do more.

Then, in around October 2016, I crashed. Crashed probably isn't the right word, but one day, I went to work, looked around at what I had on and what I had to do, felt very flat and declared, "I don't want to be a lawyer anymore". I looked at the piles and piles of work, files mounting, the demands on me from my team, questions to be answered, things to be approved and had no desire, no drive, no nothing to do anything. I had some days at home. I saw a psychologist for a while. I thought something was wrong with me. I bought books with titles like "You're so smart, why aren't you happy". You see, the logical person in me thought this was silly; get over it, just get started; you are not this person.

After a long reflection, I now know that I was burnt out. I'd been working in the same job for the same firm for 11 years. Regular employees would have 8 to 9 weeks of paid long service leave. I stopped being an employee in 2009, 7 years earlier. I threw myself into the business and just kept going. I was exhausted.

In his 2021 book *Burnout: A Guide to Identifying Burnout and Pathways to Recovery*, Gordon Parker says that burnout is distinctly overrepresented in dutiful, reliable, conscientious, and often perfectionistic people. These people are more likely to stay at work for longer hours and stay on after they are supposed to leave. As you go up the hierarchy, your chance of burnout increases.

The research undertaken by Parker and his team expanded on traditional models and measurements for burnout. Burnout's definition rests on three key symptoms as described in the World Health Organisations ICD-11 manual:

- Energy depletion and exhaustion;
- Increased mental disturbance from one's job or feelings of negativism and cynicism related to one's job; and
- Reduced professional efficacy.

In their research, Parker and team found that burnout is a constellation of symptoms beyond these three domains. They also discovered that burnout is not just limited to those in formal work positions, and they were able to link a heightened risk of burnout to those with a particular personality style. The research noted:

- Exhaustion is a central component.
- There is a loss of empathy, but for many, this symptom is experienced more broadly as a general inability to feel or a loss of *joie de vivre.*
- There is compromised work performance – though what underlies it is still to be determined – likely to be decreased by pervasive exhaustion, exacerbated by decreased motivation and or impaired concentration, perhaps all three.
- Impaired cognition emerged as a central characteristic of burnout – difficulty concentrating, needing to re-read things, failing to capture the meaning the first time, lowered attention span, poor memory, distractibility and when reading, tending to scan rather than being able to focus.
- Perfectionism heightens the risk of burnout – perfectionistic individuals set very high standards for themselves and are self-critical when they perceive they have failed. They are usually highly dutiful and reliable; they cope with pressure by working harder and harder.

Now, in addition to this "I don't want to be a lawyer anymore" and the loss of any feeling or joy about my work, I developed a severe eye issue.

As part of my business accelerator, I accepted the challenge to write a book – 30,000 words in 30 days.

Over a weekend in August 2016, I wrote 15,000 words, which involved detailed computer work. My eyes were sore and bruised, and my vision was very cloudy. I thought I had overdone it and strained my eyes – too much computer work.

What happened was an acute stress event causing the discovery of what I now know to be something called Iritis, which is an inflammation around the iris. Lots of testing later and a new relationship with a great ophthalmologist, I now know that I have a genetic predisposition to this flare-up. For me, it shows up in my body when I am stressed. It's almost like my eyes know it before my brain catches on. My eye feels bruised, the whites go red, and my vision is blurred. The treatment is a long course of steroid drops, left untreated, a steroid injection to the eye – which, thankfully, so far, I've avoided! If that isn't an incentive to take the drops, I don't know what is.

So now, when I reflect on my 2016 experience, I can see:

- I was exhausted.
- I had that loss of empathy – no joy for life or work and many, many hours staring into space.
- I didn't want to go to work, and there is no doubt my work suffered.
- I wasn't sleeping.
- Physically, this genetic predisposition to Iritis showed up.

I think labels help sometimes. Reflecting back and knowing I was burnt out helped me understand what I was going through. Otherwise, I was a pretty intelligent, logical person who thought something more sinister was happening.

Recently, I started to feel something similar. I think time was going too fast, and the demands on me were getting too much – I found myself getting sassy too quickly. I was short with my team in communications, and I know that is not me. And my eyes flared again. I knew it was time for some 'time out' to reset and refocus.

Because it impacts everything when you are that tired. You have no energy on weekends, no energy to work on the projects that bring you joy, and no energy for your family or friends; you withdraw within yourself.

You have nothing but exhaustion, and that's no way to live.

So why share this with you in a positive book about how you can thrive as a lawyer? Why start here in the doom and gloom of mental health and burnout? The reality is that if you do not set yourself up for success from the start, if you do not know these things and do not know what to look out for, it can happen to you. All that hard work to get to where you are can be out the window if you don't look after yourself, see the warning signs and take a step back or pause.

Of course, there are those of you who will say, "that won't happen to me," and that's okay. With the stats mentioned earlier in the introduction, the odds are it may happen to someone you know, so you will know what to look out for in your mates and colleagues to ensure they are okay.

Ultimately, this book aims to set you up for success. It encourages you to take specific, strategic steps to give yourself the best opportunity to excel in your legal career. In this book, you will find key skills and knowledge to help you bridge the gap between law school theory and real-life legal practice.

In **Chapter 1**, we'll walk through the transition from theory to practice, welcoming you to the real world of legal practice. We cover mastering time, setting realistic expectations and embracing positivity. **Chapter 2** builds on those foundations with sections on the profession, ethics, billable hours, mindset and more.

Chapter 3 wanders into the mythical world of work-life balance and provides a pathway to work-life harmony and a guide to looking after your body, mind, and spirit in what can be a relentless profession.

In **Chapter 4**, we learn about the culture of law practice, how to build relationships, embrace time management, handle feedback and celebrate achievements.

Chapter 5 discusses the importance of effective communication, understanding the art of silence, asking good questions, and communicating effectively.

Analysing the need for a new job or simply a new challenge is the topic of **Chapter 6**. We will work through how to know when it is time for a change and navigate the transition. We also dive into managing your professional brand, networking and the power of mentorship.

Chapter 7 is about learning every day, both within the boundaries of the law and beyond.

In **Chapter 8**, we wrap up with a bonus tip on kindness in law. Kindness to others and kindness to yourself are vital if we are to survive and thrive in legal practice.

We'll round out the book with some concluding thoughts in the **Conclusion** and a **Resources** section, which sets out the specific references referred to in the book (for example, the links to the studies referred to in the introduction can be found in the Resources section).

My ultimate goal in writing this book and sharing this information with you is to provide you with a strong foundation for a long, happy, balanced legal career.

Practical Exercises

Becoming a successful lawyer is about more than mastering legal principles and courtroom strategies. It goes beyond the textbooks and precedents, delving into experience, self-awareness, and personal growth. The art of reflection is one indispensable element that shapes the path to becoming a proficient lawyer. For those reasons, in each chapter of this book, you will find practical exercises relevant to the chapter to emphasise the importance of reflection in becoming a more effective and impactful legal professional.

Hughes, Ginnett, and Curphy state in *Leadership: Enhancing the Lessons of Experience* that making the most of experience is critical to developing one's abilities. The authors note, "Experiential learning theorists, such as Kolb, believe people learn more from their experiences when they spend time thinking about them".

These ideas extend to what Hughes, Ginnett, and Curphy note as the **action-observation-reflection (A-0-R) model**, which shows that leadership development is enhanced when the experience involves three processes: action, observation, and reflection.

I believe **reflection is the most crucial aspect** of this model and a necessity for your growth as a lawyer. It is the process through which you transform experiences into lessons, challenges into opportunities, and setbacks into stepping stones. By embracing the power of reflection and actively engaging in the practical exercises provided, you will become a more skilful lawyer and a more self-aware, adaptable, and resilient legal professional.

Other Things to Know About This Book

There are some essential things to know about how I have written this book. I hope that it will be helpful wherever you practice law in the world.

Around the world, legal practitioners have different titles: Lawyer, Solicitor, Barrister, Advocate, Attorney, Counsellor, Counsel, Prosecutor, Public Defender, and District Attorney. In this book, I have chosen the word **Lawyer**, which is generally understood to be associated with the practice of law.

Note that this book is written as an information guide only. It should not be read as advice specific to your personal circumstances. This is particularly relevant when we are dealing with topics related to mental health, stress, anxiety and burnout. I am not a medical practitioner. This book does not contain medical advice. If you feel like you are suffering from any of the symptoms referred to in this book, you should consult with a medical practitioner and obtain advice about your individual circumstances.

Finally, **the grammar and formatting in this book are in Australian English**. That means – no "z", the occasional "u" thrown in, and some other letters doubled or in a different order. The principles are the same; the words mean the same. Go with it.

It is on that basis that I hope you find this helpful book. What you will discover in this book is information in a format you can understand to equip you to make good decisions early within your legal career to set you up for the best possible career in the legal profession.

Chapter 1:

You are not in Kansas anymore: Welcome to the Real World

The legal profession is a noble and demanding calling, attracting individuals driven by a deep sense of justice and a passion for making a difference in the lives of others. Yet, like any pursuit, a legal career has its challenges and pitfalls. In these moments, when things don't go as planned, lawyers are truly tested, and their resilience is forged.

Just as Dorothy in "The Wizard of Oz" finds herself in a fantastic world far from Kansas, new lawyers enter the legal world markedly different from their law school environment. It's a transition from theory to practice, where the stakes are real, and the challenges are substantial.

The legal profession is not just about knowing the law; it's about applying it in the real world, where cases are not neatly confined to textbooks, and clients' lives hang in the balance. It's about mastering the art of time, where every second counts and deadlines can be unforgiving. And it's about navigating the myriad challenges that come your way, from demanding clients to complex cases.

As a fresh graduate, stepping into the legal profession is an exciting and transformative journey. You've conquered law school and aced your exams, and now it's time to apply your knowledge in the real world. However, this transition from theory to practice is not without its challenges. Many new lawyers find themselves in unfamiliar territory, facing the complexities of actual legal cases and the demands of clients, their bosses and colleagues. Then there is the need to appear before a Judge and make some form of articulate argument or submission! It can be overwhelming.

One of the first hurdles to overcome is the realisation that legal practice isn't always as straightforward as the textbooks made it seem. In practice, client work is rarely black and white. There are several shades of grey and sometimes all the colours of the rainbow. All of your work will require your careful consideration and judgment. You'll encounter clients with diverse needs and expectations, each presenting unique challenges. Moreover, the legal profession operates on tight schedules, demanding long hours and precise time management. It's a profession that demands meticulous attention to detail, impeccable organisation, and a mastery of time.

As you will see in this book, mastering time is more than timesheets and productivity. It's about finding the right balance for you in your work and life as you manage your job as a lawyer, deadlines and client expectations, all while going to the gym, eating well, sleeping well and avoiding burnout.

It's a fine line to tread, but it's essential for maintaining your well-being and effectiveness as a lawyer. Equally crucial is your mindset and attitude. Maintaining a growth mindset, cultivating resilience, and staying positive during the inevitable challenges of your early career can be the difference between thriving and merely surviving. So, let's dive into the strategies and insights to help you adapt to the real world of law and thrive in it, all while maintaining your passion for the profession.

FROM THEORY TO PRACTICE: NAVIGATING THE REAL WORLD OF LAW

Picture yourself as a student, eagerly absorbing legal theories and principles in the hallowed halls of your law school. The professors present you with intricate legal concepts, and you diligently pore over cases, attempting to decipher the nuances of the legal landscape. It's an intellectual journey into the theoretical world of law.

But then, the real world of legal practice hits you like a strong gust of wind. On your first day on the job, you realise that while law school equipped you with knowledge, it didn't quite prepare you for the practical rigours of being a lawyer. In anticipation of your brilliance, your boss expects you to be more seasoned than your "Day 1" status might suggest.

Think of it this way: theoretical knowledge is like watching a video tutorial on bike riding. You can study it exhaustively, absorbing all the steps and strategies. You might even imagine yourself navigating various paths on that bike. But here's the catch: no matter how many hours you dedicate to that video, you will only become a skilled cyclist once you get on the bike and start pedalling.

Once you're on that bike, the real learning begins. Balancing, pedalling with the proper force, and making sharp turns take practice and patience. Over time, you evolve from a hesitant novice to a confident rider, capable of making split-second decisions and conquering terrains that once seemed daunting.

The legal profession follows a similar trajectory. The theoretical knowledge you gather in lecture halls equips you with the foundational understanding needed to tackle legal challenges. This knowledge is indispensable; you must master it while staying updated with new developments.

However, like the bike, you must also acquire practical skills to successfully navigate the intricate, competitive legal industry. These skills include:

- **Networking:** Building connections is crucial in the legal world.
- **Self-care:** Learning to take care of your physical and mental well-being.
- **Navigating toxic environments:** Strategies for dealing with challenging workplaces.
- **Addressing workplace issues:** Handling bullying, harassment, and other workplace problems.

- **Financial management:** Setting realistic salary expectations and budgeting wisely.
- **Career development:** Strategies for advancing your legal career.
- **Managing competition:** Thriving in a competitive field.
- **Budgets and timesheets:** Meeting your boss's expectations.
- **Seeking help:** Recognising when to ask for assistance or support.
- **Managing expectations:** Balancing your own expectations with those of peers and superiors.

Read that list again. I am pretty sure you won't find those topics in any law school curriculum.

Further and ideally, your legal education would lead to employment at a firm that values your growth and well-being. In reality, law schools churn out thousands of graduates every year, and someone is always waiting to take your place if you don't meet your firm's expectations. This vulnerability can lead to misuse or exploitation.

You don't have to accept this fate. As the saying goes, "forewarned is forearmed." The knowledge and insights you gain from this book will arm you with the tools to navigate these complex scenarios, assert your needs confidently, build a support network, and prioritise your health and career. This knowledge will bridge the gap between theory and practice, setting the stage for your success in the challenging yet immensely rewarding world of law.

NAVIGATING CHALLENGES IN THE LEGAL PROFESSION

So, what are some of the practical challenges the legal profession faces? In my many years of law, there are some key themes for where things go wrong for lawyers. From going nowhere in their careers, making mistakes, damaging their professional reputation, or worse, disciplinary actions. While those practical aspects are important, mental health issues and burnout are two equally important, critical factors that impact legal careers.

Going Nowhere

The desire for progress and advancement in a legal career is a common aspiration. Lawyers often enter the profession with ambitious goals, hoping to make their mark, climb the ranks, and achieve professional success. However, the path to success is not always straightforward, and some pitfalls can lead to career stagnation.

Sometimes, a plateau in a legal career might not be your fault. You may have always worked where you've worked and not experienced anything else. You may also be very happy doing what you are doing. Generally, though, most new lawyers are ambitious and keen to excel and prove their worth to colleagues.

Some factors that hold lawyers back include not putting their hand up when the opportunity to step up presents itself or not having confidence in their ability to take the next step. Not keeping up with professional development and the latest rules, laws, and trends can mean that you are behind when it comes to your peers.

Making Mistakes

The perceived busy, busy nature of law and work means that you might feel like you have so much to do and not enough time to do it. It is a constant battle. If you keep saying yes to new things to get ahead and impress your boss, you might find yourself in too deep and totally overwhelmed.

It is in this environment that mistakes happen and happen often. It can be as simple as not proofreading an email before it is sent with silly typos, to missing a critical date, or miscommunicating your client's instructions.

Mistakes have varying consequences – from embarrassment to disciplinary proceedings. Further, Clients expect high-quality legal services. They may become dissatisfied if they perceive a lack of competence, attention to detail, or dedication in their lawyer's work – making it a problem for you, your boss, and potentially your career.

Your Professional Reputation

Your professional reputation is a priceless asset, often regarded as the currency of trust. It sets the stage for your career: building bridges with clients, colleagues, and the judiciary. Like an intricately woven tapestry, your reputation is crafted from the threads of your competence, ethics, and integrity. Once these threads are damaged, it becomes a challenging, uphill journey to mend what's been broken.

Picture this: a courtroom where every lawyer is a character in an elaborate play. Your reputation is your script, your lines whispered among colleagues and Judges, spoken in the quiet corridors of courthouses, and echoed through the chambers of law firms. The role you play in the legal drama defines whether you're seen as a protagonist, a villain, or merely an extra in the background.

A tarnished reputation can turn even the most brilliant legal minds into the sceptics' gallery, casting shadows of doubt on your every word and action. And **while building a reputation can be a lifelong endeavour, losing it can happen in the blink of an eye**. That's why safeguarding your professional standing should be a constant, unwavering commitment because once lost, it's akin to trying to unring a bell in the minds of those who matter most in your legal career.

Disciplinary Proceedings

Ethics and our professional codes of conduct are the bedrock upon which the profession stands. As a lawyer, you are entrusted with a special responsibility to uphold the highest ethical standards, ensuring that justice is served and clients' rights are protected. Above all, you have a duty to the Court and the administration of justice.

The desire for success and the pressure to win cases can sometimes lead lawyers to cut ethical corners in pursuit of victory. Failure to identify, disclose, or manage conflicts of interest can result in ethical violations that harm clients' interests. Providing false or misleading information in Court or during negotiations can lead to allegations of unethical conduct. Failing to fulfil obligations to clients, such as neglecting cases or abandoning clients, can breach ethical duties. Unauthorised disclosure of confidential client information is a grave ethical violation.

Not only will this conduct impact your professional reputation, but it will likely lead to disciplinary proceedings, significantly impacting your ability to continue as a lawyer.

Your Mental Health Matters

In the day-to-day thrust of law, where arguments are waged with words and cases are carried on broad shoulders, there's an unspoken battle many lawyers fight silently – the struggle for mental health. It's a paradoxical world where, on one side, lawyers are looked upon as stalwarts of strength and reason, while on the other, the statistics reveal a chilling truth. Anxiety, depression, and mental health challenges quietly haunt the corridors of law firms and courtrooms.

There's a certain stigma that veils the topic of mental health in the legal profession. An unspoken code of keeping up appearances persists, where a facade of strength is often worn as armour. Many lawyers bear their burdens alone, reluctant to admit vulnerability, fearing it might tarnish their professional image. Yet, the importance of safeguarding your mental health can't be overstated. The relentless pace, high stakes, and the weight of others' burdens all conspire to cast shadows on the brightest minds. Acknowledging the importance of mental well-being is not a sign of weakness but rather an affirmation of the strength required to weather the storms that come with a legal career.

The Peril of Burnout

The legal profession is notorious for its demanding nature, with long hours, high-pressure cases, and complex legal matters. While dedication and hard work are often celebrated virtues in this field, there's a fine line between commitment and burnout. Burnout, a state of emotional, physical, and mental exhaustion, is an ever-present danger for lawyers, particularly when their careers don't start well, lack strong foundations, and fail to incorporate proper self-care and time management practices.

If you find yourself taking on excessive cases and responsibilities, it can lead to long working hours and relentless stress. The legal profession's demands can leave little room for personal life, leading to a lack of relaxation and rejuvenation. You may neglect self-care practices, including exercise, healthy eating, and adequate sleep, exacerbating burnout symptoms. The constant pressure of deadlines, the emotional toll of challenging cases, and client expectations can contribute to chronic stress. Setting boundaries with clients, colleagues, and superiors may be difficult, leading to an "always on" mentality.

Burnout doesn't just impact a lawyer's well-being; it can have profound consequences on their career, clients, and overall quality of life. Burnout can impair cognitive function and decision-making, leading to a decrease in the quality of legal work. You may struggle to meet deadlines, communicate effectively, or provide the level of service your clients expect, leading to client dissatisfaction. Burnout can manifest in physical health problems, including sleep disorders, increased susceptibility to illness, and chronic fatigue. You are at a higher risk of mental health issues, such as anxiety and depression. Burnout can hinder career progression, as you may lack the energy and motivation to take on new challenges or seek growth opportunities.

Don't despair; it's not all doom and gloom

There are some simple steps you can take or things to keep in mind to set you up with good foundations to avoid these things. It won't surprise you that these are key themes and topics in this book.

From the outset, **establish clear and realistic expectations with clients** regarding case outcomes, timelines, and communication. Maintain **open, transparent, and regular communication** with clients. Keep them informed about case progress and address their concerns promptly.

Diligently research, prepare, and represent clients to ensure the **highest quality of legal service** every single day. Attention to detail and competence can go a long way in preventing dissatisfaction.

Safeguard client **confidentiality** at all costs and ensure that no unauthorised disclosures occur. Carefully identify, disclose, and **manage conflicts of interest** to avoid compromising client interests. **Uphold the highest standards of honesty and integrity** in all professional interactions, regardless of what you see others doing. If something feels wrong, don't do it. **Seek guidance from mentors**, colleagues, or ethics committees to ensure compliance with ethical rules.

Set realistic workloads, be mindful of your capacity, and avoid overloading yourself with cases and responsibilities. If your boss keeps allocating files, have good conversations about what work needs to take priority. Make time for **exercise, healthy eating, adequate sleep**, and relaxation to recharge your physical and mental batteries. **Set boundaries** with clients, colleagues, and superiors to ensure that work doesn't consume your entire life. **Seek support** from mentors, colleagues, or mental health professionals if you struggle with burnout.

Embrace a **mindset of continuous learning**. Invest time in acquiring new skills, staying updated with legal developments, and seeking opportunities for professional growth. Don't underestimate the value of mentorship. **Reach out to experienced lawyers who can provide guidance**, share their experiences, and help you navigate the complexities of the legal profession.

Build and nurture a strong professional network. Networking can open doors to new opportunities, collaborations, and career advancements. Attend legal events, join professional associations, and engage with colleagues. **Define your career goals** and create a roadmap for achieving them. Regularly assess your progress and adjust your strategies as needed.

MASTERING TIME: YOUR MOST PRECIOUS ASSET

Time is your greatest treasure, a currency more valuable than gold. It's a resource you must not only cherish but wield with precision. As a lawyer, your days are a complex tapestry of tasks and responsibilities, each demanding your attention and expertise. Picture a typical day where you might find yourself:

- Providing legal counsel to clients seeking your guidance.
- Engaging in constant communication with clients, ensuring they are informed and supported.
- Diving deep into legal research.
- Crafting meticulous legal documents that can sway the tides of justice.
- Stepping into courtrooms, representing clients with unwavering determination.

- Drafting pleadings and applications, the building blocks of legal battles.
- Being ready to travel at a moment's notice, a suitcase always ready.
- Staying vigilant, keeping pace with ever-evolving legal regulations and statutory landscape.
- Poring over cases and practice updates, extracting the wisdom essential to your work.
- And then the phone rings or your boss calls you into their office – a crisis has occurred, and an urgent matter requires you to drop everything you are already managing.

Each task has its own deadlines, often of the "tick-tock" variety. Balancing multiple cases, each with its own clock counting down, requires finesse.

Adding to the complexity, the legal world often operates on a time-based model. Time is not merely a factor; it's an essential term interwoven into the fabric of legal principles. **The consequences of mismanaging time can be far-reaching and detrimental** for you and your clients.

Missed deadlines don't just cause ripples; they can send shockwaves through your client's case. Imagine missing a discovery or disclosure deadline, a misstep that might lead to losing crucial evidence. Missing a limitation period could rob your client of their right to pursue a claim. Worse yet, these lapses can open the door to complaints that question your competence, casting a shadow over your reputation and potentially ending your legal career.

In reality, missing deadlines doesn't make your work easier; it makes it infinitely more complicated. The domino effect kicks in as you scramble to reschedule while taking on new cases. Stress, anxiety, and even depression can follow, casting a dark cloud over your career.

So, how can you navigate these relentless time constraints and keep the clock from becoming your enemy? Here are some strategies:

- Don't take on new clients when your plate is overflowing. Prioritise the work that you have committed to. Talk to your boss or manager about what work needs priority when new work comes in.
- Avoid procrastinating. Address tasks promptly, even those you'd rather avoid.
- Don't be a lone wolf; learn to delegate wisely to your team or assistant.
- Never bite off more than you can chew; manage your workload and communicate with senior lawyers to prioritise tasks.
- Leverage time recording, calendar management, and document-building software.
- Be realistic when estimating how long it will take you to complete a task to avoid overcommitting.
- Silence notifications and create focus zones to shield yourself from distractions and interruptions.
- Strive for excellence, not unattainable perfection; trust yourself to do your work well (this topic could be a whole book all on its own).

These things can work in an ideal world where you control everything you do. You rarely have that control when you work for someone, especially as a new lawyer. **Communication is your biggest ally here**. Prioritise your commitments, and if you need help with managing what you have, talk to your team leader, manager, or boss about what needs to be prioritised. Don't underestimate how long it will take to do something – we all do it daily: "Sure, it will just take me 30 minutes to draft these orders." … 1 hour later … Work out your estimate, add a buffer, and communicate well.

Work out if others in your team can assist you – do you have a legal assistant or paralegal – these are your best chances of getting things done. When you are a new lawyer, your legal assistant or paralegal will likely know more than you do and know how to do what you need to do more efficiently than you can. Learn from them and ask for help. Communicate well.

Procrastination

There are those magical people out there who dive in and do what they need to do. Then there are the mere mortals like the rest of us who avoid the hard tasks, leave them until last, and then it's urgent. And then, unsurprisingly, you do the task, and you think – "Well, that wasn't as bad as I thought, feels good, why did I wait to do that".

A great friend (and a former office manager) used to say – "come on, Elizabeth, eat that frog". I am, at times, very good at avoiding the frog (just a mere mortal, after all).

Brian Tracy's book *Eat That Frog* introduces the concept of the "frog" as a metaphor for the most important, challenging, and often procrastinated task of the day. As a new lawyer, you'll likely encounter a barrage of tasks and responsibilities daily. Some may be enticing, while others are less appealing but crucial for your growth and success. It's these critical tasks that Tracy calls "frogs."

The central idea is to tackle your most important and challenging task – the "frog" – early in the day. Doing so will give you a sense of accomplishment and set a positive tone for the rest of the day.

That makes sense, right? But how do we do that? It all comes down to mindset and setting yourself up with good practices and routines to carry you through your career. The more you cement these things now, in your early years, the more likely they will become second nature to you. You will walk into the office each day and know that your day starts with the "frog" task, and everything flows from there.

How do you know which tasks are the "frog" tasks? Firstly, I expect your gut will tell you. If you have a task you've been putting off and an impending sense of doom when you think about it, that is your "frog" task.

Tracy introduces a straightforward method for prioritising tasks: the ABCDE method. This approach might help you differentiate between essential and less critical tasks.

- **A Tasks:** These are your top priorities, often the "frogs" that must be eaten first.
- **B Tasks:** These are important but not as critical as A tasks.
- **C Tasks:** These are tasks with minor consequences, often tasks you can delegate.
- **D Tasks:** These are tasks you can delegate without any repercussions.
- **E Tasks:** These are tasks that you can eliminate altogether; they don't contribute significantly to your goals.

If you have a task list – an ongoing to-do list or tasks generated by your practice management software – print it out and work through it. It is also essential to work through your calendar – if you have not prepared for your upcoming court appearance in the coming days, that needs to be on your list.

Tracy emphasises the importance of focusing on time management. You often find yourself juggling multiple cases, meetings, and deadlines. To stay productive, minimising distractions and maintaining concentrated effort is crucial.

- **Single-tasking:** Rather than multitasking, focus on one task at a time. It improves efficiency and reduces errors.
- **Time blocking:** Allocate specific blocks of time to certain tasks or categories of work. This helps create a structured schedule.
- **Eliminate distractions:** Identify common distractions (e.g., excessive email checking or social media) and minimise them during focused work periods.
- **Use technology wisely:** Use productivity tools and apps to streamline tasks and track progress.

The art of mastering procrastination is akin to wielding a magic wand. Navigating competing priorities, embracing communication as your greatest ally, and resisting the siren call of procrastination are all essential skills on this journey. As Brian Tracy said, "Eat That Frog!" – tackle your most challenging tasks head-on, and you'll find your days more productive and your sense of accomplishment soaring.

We'll come back to this topic in Chapter 3.

SETTING REALISTIC EXPECTATIONS

As you begin your career in law, you will no doubt be thinking about where your career will go and what you can achieve. I have heard many junior lawyers have "make partner" as their goal from the outset without a fundamental understanding of what that means. For most people, their career path goes something like this:

- Summer associate;
- Paralegal;
- Lawyer
- Associate Lawyer;

- Senior Lawyer;
- Special Counsel;
- Law firm partner or Legal Practice Director.

Whatever your goals, it is important to be realistic both in what they are and how you will achieve those goals. Keep in mind that, like many in the legal profession, if you are a high achiever, a-type personality or perfectionist (or whichever labels society might define), the reality is that you are likely to feel stuck, even if you are moving forward. Maki Moussavi notes in her book *The High Achievers Guide: Transform Your Success Mindset and Begin the Quest to Fulfillment* that this is often because you are living your life according to societal definitions of success rather than your own. Your mindset is critical to how you define success.

As a new lawyer, it's crucial to grasp the reality that progression in your legal career is not an automatic conveyor belt leading to success. Your progression is unlikely to be based on the years you have worked, with an automated pay increase each year. This understanding is vital for several reasons.

The legal profession highly values **merit and competence**. It's not about how long you've been practising; it's about the quality of your work, dedication, and ability to deliver results.

Becoming a skilled lawyer requires more than just years of service. It takes **commitment to continuous learning**, honing your skills, and adapting to the ever-evolving legal landscape.

Automatic progression can lead to complacency. When you have to work hard and prove your abilities for each step forward, **you remain motivated to excel**. Complacency can hinder your personal and professional development.

Unrealistic expectations can lead to frustration and disappointment.

Understanding that progression requires effort can help you set more achievable goals and avoid unnecessary stress.

To keep your expectations in check while progressing forward, first and foremost - **do the work, do good work, consistently**.

Define clear, achievable **short-term and long-term goals**. Break down your career aspirations into manageable steps, and celebrate your accomplishments along the way.

Request **feedback from mentors, colleagues, and supervisors** regularly. Constructive feedback can provide insights into your strengths and areas for improvement.

Commit to **continuous learning and skill development**. Attend seminars, workshops, and CLE programs to stay updated with legal trends and refine your expertise.

Build a professional network with mentors and experienced lawyers who can offer guidance. Networking can open doors to opportunities for growth and advancement.

Understand that career progression may take time. **Patience is a valuable virtue in the legal profession**. Focus on your journey rather than rushing to reach the destination. Moussavi notes that "success isn't about reaching a destination; it's about enjoying the journey."

Acknowledge and **celebrate your achievements**, no matter how small they may seem. Recognising your progress can boost motivation and maintain a positive outlook.

Remember, by embracing hard work, dedication, and realistic expectations, you will progress and build a fulfilling and enduring career in law.

EMBRACING POSITIVITY: ATTITUDE IS EVERYTHING

When challenges and high-pressure situations are commonplace in the legal profession, maintaining a positive mindset is not just a luxury – it's a necessity. *The Art of Possibility* by Rosamund Zander and Benjamin Zander offers valuable insights into how positivity can transform your legal career and life. It's also one of the most beautiful books to listen to (the audible version is highly recommended). Benjamin Zander was the conductor of the Boston Philharmonic, and the incorporation of music into the audible text is delightful.

"The Art of Possibility" encourages a shift from a scarcity mindset, where challenges seem impossible, to a mindset of abundance and possibility. Embracing this abundance mindset provides for, in my view, a career that is filled with opportunity.

Positivity opens the door to **creative problem-solving**. Instead of fixating on obstacles, you'll explore innovative solutions to legal issues.

A positive outlook **strengthens your resilience** in the face of setbacks. You'll bounce back from challenges with newfound determination. Positivity **fosters better communication** with colleagues, clients, and opposing parties. It promotes collaboration and conflict resolution. Viewing each situation as an opportunity for growth encourages **continuous learning and improvement**.

When you adopt a positive mindset, you will see potential in every situation. Positivity fuels confidence, inspires creative problem-solving, and attracts opportunities. Learn to reframe challenges as opportunities. Instead of seeing an obstacle, ask, "What's possible here?" Focus on how you can contribute to your team, organisation, or clients. Shifting from self-concern to contribution enhances positivity. Acknowledge your achievements, no matter how small. Celebrating wins creates a positive feedback loop.

Maintaining a positive outlook isn't about living in a world devoid of challenges or difficulties. It's about approaching these obstacles with resilience and a constructive attitude. I acknowledge that the legal profession can present tough days, demanding cases, and high-stress situations. I am not proposing an alternate Pollyanna reality where everything is perpetually rosy. Indeed, there will be moments when maintaining positivity might seem overwhelmingly daunting. However, in the grand scheme of your legal career, a positive mindset becomes one of your most valuable assets.

By adopting a positive attitude, you equip yourself with the mental fortitude needed to navigate the complex terrain of the legal world. Challenges become growth opportunities, setbacks transform into stepping stones, and adversity becomes the fuel that propels you forward. While there may be occasional tough days, maintaining an overall positive outlook helps weather the storms.

PRACTICAL EXERCISES

Reflection is a powerful tool for learning, personal growth, and professional development. It deepens our understanding, enhances critical thinking, reinforces learning, and equips us with valuable skills for navigating life's challenges and opportunities. With that in mind, here are some practical exercises that you can use to reflect on the themes of Chapter 1:

1. **Legal Realism Reflection:** Take some time to reflect on the transition from law school to legal practice. Write down your expectations and fears. Consider what you believe the most significant challenges might be. This exercise will help you clarify your mindset as you enter the real world of law.

2. **Career Path Mapping:** Take time to map out your career goals and aspirations. Identify potential paths within the legal profession, such as litigation, corporate law, public interest, or academia. Consider the skills and experiences required for each path.
3. **Mentorship Quest:** Reach out to a legal professional, whether a professor, practising lawyer, or someone in a legal-related role. Request a conversation or meeting to discuss their experiences transitioning from law school to the legal profession. This firsthand insight can be invaluable in preparing you for the journey ahead.

Incorporating regular reflection into our learning and decision-making processes can lead to more meaningful and effective outcomes in our personal and professional lives.

CONCLUSION

In this opening chapter, we've explored the challenges you can encounter when you misunderstand the transition from law student to lawyer or neglect the fundamental elements required for success in the legal profession. We have worked through time mastery, expectations and the need to remain positive. My key points are these:

- Time is a resource you must cherish and wield with precision.
- Eat the "frog" and tackle your most important and challenging task early in the day. Make this a habit early in your career.
- Progression in your legal career is not an automatic conveyor belt leading to success. Do the work, do good work, communicate well and prove your worth.
- Positivity fuels confidence, inspires creative problem-solving, and attracts opportunities.

What are your key takeaways? Make a note, get a sticky note, highlight, and keep reflecting on how you can incorporate key themes that resonate with you into your daily life.

One of the defining questions that every lawyer should ponder is: **What kind of lawyer do you aspire to be?** This isn't just a casual query; it's the compass that will guide your legal career, dictating the path you will travel, the cases you'll champion, and the lives you'll touch.

What about you? What do you want to do? Only you can determine what you're passionate about.

Are you passionate about helping families or people going through a divorce – become a family lawyer. Perhaps you want to help people in trouble with the law and become a criminal lawyer. Maybe you are passionate about keeping our roads safe or the environment or you love working your way through complex documents. Determine what that something is, and then do your best to become the best lawyer you can be.

In the early stages of your career you might not know what you want to focus on or specialise in, and that's okay too. Learn about different areas, attend conferences or training that cover multiple areas, sit in on different topics to get a feel for each area. It may also be that you are in a rural area and a good grasp of general practice is necessary. Find what works for you.

Achieving your professional goals will require a strong foundation right from the start. You can develop that foundation by working through the concepts in this chapter.

The path won't always be smooth, and challenges will undoubtedly arise. Yet, through these trials and tribulations, you will grow, evolve, and emerge as the lawyer you've envisioned.

UNDERSTANDING THE LEGAL PROFESSION

If you want to develop a strong foundation for your career in law, the first thing you need to do is understand what the legal profession is all about.

The legal profession has been around for centuries. At this point, you are probably thinking, "Yeah, yeah, I just studied this. I get it".

I think it's worth repeating and remembering why we do what we do as lawyers and why it is such an important profession. There will be days when something will happen – the pressure might be high, you see other lawyers acting in a certain way, you miss one thing and then another. It's a slippery slope when things start to go wrong, and it is for those reasons that this section is a must-read.

Many countries have unique laws and a judiciary charged with interpreting those laws and passing judgment. However, lawyers play a crucial role in interpreting laws since their words can influence judicial decisions.

That's not a simple task. This is why we have legislation, rules and codes of conduct that we must follow along with bar associations, law societies and professional bodies to manage that. The driving purpose is to ensure that lawyers maintain the utmost integrity when dealing with the law.

For example, an Australian solicitor's primary duties are to the Court and the administration of justice. In addition, solicitors need to:

- Act in their client's best interest.
- Be honest and polite when dealing with professional engagements.
- Deliver legal services promptly, professionally, and conscientiously.
- Follow the rules of practice provided by the Australian Solicitors Conduct Rules.

The legal profession has strict regulations because civilisation may cease to exist without regulation and social responsibility. As such, it is up to each lawyer to familiarise themselves with the code of conduct that governs lawyers in their country.

THE UNYIELDING IMPORTANCE OF PROFESSIONAL COURTESY

In the intricate dance of legal practice, where every move can impact not just cases but the profession's reputation as a whole, understanding and embodying professional courtesy is integral to the profession's future.

"Do unto others as you would have them do unto you."

When you are courteous and respectful toward other practitioners, support staff, clients, other parties, Judges, and the security guard at the Court, you not only uphold the profession's dignity but also fortify your own reputation. It's a two-way street – your demeanour toward others sets the tone for how you can expect to be treated, irrespective of your seniority or perceived brilliance.

It's easy to look around and emulate the behaviours you see, especially if superiors or colleagues indulge in less-than-courteous conduct. However, wisdom dictates that you should resist this temptation. In a world where professionalism often teeters on the precipice, exercising discernment is vital. The simplicity of basic courtesies, such as "please" and "thank you," shouldn't be underestimated. These age-old gestures still carry weight, providing the scaffolding for healthy professional relationships.

Remember that your Solicitors' Conduct Rules serve as the ultimate guide for professional conduct. Knowing and understanding these ethical obligations is your compass in navigating the often tumultuous seas of legal practice.

Discrimination, dishonesty, and disrespect have no place in the lexicon of professional courtesy. Your interactions with fellow practitioners should never descend into intimidation, threats, offence, or insults. A commitment to clear and respectful communication, whether in correspondence or discussions, is essential to professional courtesy. Additionally, punctuality and responsiveness in returning calls and correspondence form the foundations of trust within the profession.

As a new lawyer, remember that you're not just entering a profession; you're becoming a part of a legacy with much to be proud of and much to uphold.

Professional courtesy remains a steadfast ally in day-to-day legal practice where challenges are abundant, and expectations run high. It elevates the profession and cultivates an environment where respect, trust, and ethical conduct are the cornerstones of success.

ETHICS IS COOL: LEARN TO LOVE IT

As a new lawyer embarking on your journey in the legal profession, one of the most fundamental principles to internalise is the unwavering commitment to ethical conduct. The legal field is not just about mastering statutes and case law; it's about serving justice with integrity and trust. Lawyers hold a unique position in society, entrusted with the responsibility to advocate for justice and the rule of law. This privilege has a corresponding duty to always uphold the highest ethical standards.

Susan Liautaud's book *The Power of Ethics* discusses the notion that ethics is not a hindrance but a source of power and influence. High ethical standards do not constrain your legal practice; they are your most potent asset. They build trust with clients, colleagues, and the public, essential for a successful legal career.

Ethical dilemmas may arise in your legal career and can be challenging to navigate. However, the guiding principle should always be to do the right thing, even when difficult.

Always be truthful and transparent in your dealings. Lying or misrepresenting facts erodes trust and can have severe consequences.

Protect client confidentiality rigorously. **Confidential information should never be shared** without the client's informed consent. Be careful about things like working in public places or taking your work home.

Act with integrity in every aspect of your practice. Uphold moral and ethical principles, even when faced with pressure or temptation.

Be fair and just in your interactions with clients, colleagues, and opposing parties. **Treat all individuals with respect and dignity**.

Take responsibility for your actions. If a mistake is made, address it promptly and take steps to rectify it.

But others are doing it – don't follow the herd

When colleagues or competitors (even your manager or boss) engage in certain practices, it's natural to wonder whether you should do the same. However, it's crucial to remember that not all paths are ethical, and mindlessly following the herd can lead to ethical dilemmas and professional misconduct.

The **herd mentality** is a psychological phenomenon where individuals tend to conform to the actions or opinions of a larger group. In the legal field, this can manifest when lawyers observe their peers engaging in questionable practices and feel compelled to do the same, even if it goes against their ethical principles.

Following unethical practices because "everyone else is doing it" can have severe consequences. It can jeopardise your professional reputation and lead to legal and ethical violations.

To avoid falling into the trap of the herd mentality, it's essential to prioritise ethical decision-making.

Familiarise yourself with the rules of professional conduct and ethical guidelines specific to your jurisdiction. Understanding what is expected of you is the first step in making ethical decisions.

When faced with an ethical dilemma, **seek guidance from trusted mentors, colleagues, or ethics committees**. Don't hesitate to ask for advice when unsure about a particular action's ethical implications.

Your ethical principles and personal values should serve as your compass (trust your gut). If a practice goes against your principles, even if others are doing it, have the courage to take a different path.

Hold yourself accountable for your actions. If you make a mistake or realise you've engaged in unethical behaviour, take responsibility and take steps to rectify the situation.

Resisting the herd mentality is not just about avoiding unethical practices; it's also about becoming an ethical leader in your legal community. **By consistently upholding ethical standards and encouraging others to do the same, you contribute to a culture of integrity and professionalism.**

Your legacy is not just about the cases you win or the deals you close; it's about the reputation you build as an ethical and principled lawyer. Upholding high ethical standards is not optional; it's the cornerstone of your legal career. As a new lawyer, embrace the power of ethics and remember that always doing the right thing is the path to a successful and fulfilling legal practice.

MANAGE BILLABLE HOURS AND CLIENT EXPECTATIONS

As you embark on your journey within the hallowed halls of the law firm, there's a dimension of the legal world that deserves your attention – a facet that can profoundly influence your career trajectory. Welcome to the **business of law**.

Many young lawyers encounter this revelation as they progress in their careers. Initially, the focus your focus will be solely on being a lawyer, doing the work and earning an income, just by turning up each day. But as the layers of the legal profession are peeled back, a deeper understanding dawns.

Your law firm is not just a haven for legal minds; it's a business entity governed by financial structures and fiscal realities. Much like any other enterprise, it must turn a profit to sustain itself. Beneath the veneer of courtrooms and legal libraries lies a network of financial obligations. In this system, **someone must foot the bill for essentials** such as rent or mortgage payments, business and professional insurance, computers and systems, stationery and printing, and even the very desks you occupy. These are the so-called non-billable expenses – the overhead costs that keep the legal machinery humming but cannot be passed on to a client.

But that's not all. The legal profession encompasses **many activities that, while critical, don't directly translate into billable hours or immediate revenue**. These include professional development, responding to administrative emails, attending firm meetings, crafting reports, experiencing lawyer downtime, personal and sick days, managing family emergencies, savouring vacation time, engaging in administrative duties, preparing invoices, and participating in networking events. They consume precious hours yet don't contribute to the immediate bottom line.

So, where does the lifeblood of a law firm truly flow from? The answer lies in **billable hours**. This is the **life force of a law firm**, its primary source of income. It's the tangible measure of the legal services you provide to your clients – a currency that sustains the firm and fuels its growth and prosperity.

As you pursue your legal career, remember that mastering the art of billing and managing client expectations is not just about numbers; it's about understanding the **intricate dance between law and commerce**.

Picture this: you're a legal maestro, performing a symphony of services for your clients. Each note you play, whether it's drafting legal documents, engaging in client communication, composing letters, making pivotal phone calls, or delving into exhaustive research, contributes to this legal opus. These actions are not just tasks but billable endeavours. When you invest your time in them, your clients are billed accordingly.

Now, here's where the plot thickens. While law firms establish lofty expectations for their lawyers regarding billable hours, they also provide a base salary. This means a steady income stream flows into your account each month regardless of whether you meet your annual billable hours target. It's a safety net shielding you from the harsh winds of uncertainty.

Yet, tread carefully, for this financial safety net has a limit. Falling short of the expected billable hours isn't without consequences. It's like walking a tightrope; venture too far from your target and risk teetering into unemployment. Why? Because fewer billable hours translate to diminished profit for the firm, and a thriving legal enterprise relies on the harmony between effort and compensation.

But there's more to this intricate dance. Law firms have equity partners who share the reins of power and profit-sharing. They, too, generally receive a base salary, but also a share of the profits of the firm. And here's the twist – when the collective billable hours of the firm's lawyers fall short of expectations, the partners' annual earnings take a hit. In essence, the fate of every lawyer is intertwined with the firm's financial prosperity and expectations are high.

So, why do law firms set such rigorous expectations? It's not just about numbers; it's about the delicate balance between sustaining a thriving legal practice and ensuring the livelihood of every lawyer within its hallowed halls.

Billable hours will soon become an inseparable companion on

your legal journey. Picture it as the heartbeat of your legal practice, **the rhythm that defines your days**, and the foundation upon which your career is built.

Now, let's break it down. Billable hours, the sacred currency of law firms, are a variable that can range from 1700 to 2800 hours per year. It's akin to a demanding marathon where you work diligently, sometimes even clocking 70 to 80 hours a week. But here's the catch: these hours must be "billable." In other words, they should be hours directly linked to tasks and services clients are willing to pay for.

As a new lawyer, you may experience the grind of late nights and weekend toil, pouring your heart into your work, only to be told by a partner that you haven't met your billable hour target. The frustration is palpable, akin to watching your masterpiece unravel before your eyes. This is because the work you do must be good work, work of a quality that can be billed to a client. If your manager or partner has to significantly re-write the work you do, your time will be written off.

[*A pause here and a suggestion to avoid this happening to you – read client files. If you are working in a team, read the letters and documents that your partner has approved. Get a feel for the quality of the work and the language to be used. This will help you move beyond this stage.*]

Tracking your hours isn't just about appeasing the billable hour gods; it's about reclaiming control over your time. While you can't wholly avoid non-billable tasks, you have the power to streamline and economise. Delegation and automation become your allies in this battle for efficiency.

Many law firms offer practice management systems, a digital compass that records and collates your every legal endeavour. It's a tool that helps you manage your time and empowers you to see where changes are needed. Think of it as your trusted navigator through the billable hour labyrinth.

In the world of time tracking, **timesheets are your muse**. They are more than just records; they are the canvas upon which your legal journey is painted. Remember to log your time, for these sheets are the very fabric upon which your career rests.

But the billable hour tale doesn't end here. Your law firm might have other policies in play. They may engage in fixed-fee work or expect you to contribute to a monthly group budget. These variables can significantly impact your financial standing within the firm.

For instance, if you're immersed in fixed-fee work, pouring hours into it might not translate into significant financial contributions. It's a delicate balance where understanding the firm's policies and aligning your efforts accordingly becomes paramount.

As you dive into billable hours, remember that it's not just about numbers; it's about understanding the intricate symphony of time, efficiency, and fiscal realities.

THE MAGIC OF MINDSET

We started our discussion about mindset in Chapter 1 by exploring the impact a positive attitude will have on your career in law. I want to dive into this topic a little more, as how we manage our minds has a significant impact on how we manage our legal practice.

Challenges are abundant, and client expectations are high in the fast-paced world of law. Mastering your mindset is an essential component of achieving lasting success. As psychologist Carol Dweck outlined in her book, *Mindset: The New Psychology of Success*, your mindset can significantly impact your ability to thrive in your legal career. Let's delve into why understanding and managing your mindset is crucial for new lawyers.

Carol Dweck's research distinguishes between two fundamental mindsets: the fixed mindset and the growth mindset.

Individuals with a **fixed mindset** believe that their abilities, intelligence, and talents are static traits. They tend to avoid challenges, fearing failure and looking for easy, guaranteed successes. Criticism is often taken personally, leading to defensiveness. They may plateau early and never reach their full potential.

In contrast, those with a **growth mindset** perceive abilities and intelligence as malleable. They thrive on challenges, view failures as opportunities to learn, and are resilient in the face of setbacks. Criticism is seen as valuable feedback, and they continuously seek to improve and develop their skills. The growth mindset paves the way for long-term success and personal development.

If you don't go into law with a growth mindset, you'll find it hard to advance in your career. This is because a growth mindset focuses on learning and developing the skills you need to deal with whatever challenges and obstacles your career may throw your way.

Legal practice is rife with challenges – high expectations, complex cases, demanding clients, and rigorous competition. Lawyers with a growth mindset embrace these challenges as **opportunities to grow**. You can enthusiastically tackle complex cases, knowing each experience contributes to your expertise.

Not every case will end in victory. A growth mindset helps **navigate failures with resilience**. Instead of dwelling on defeat, they analyse what went wrong, learn from it, and become better equipped for future endeavours.

Successful lawyers are **lifelong learners**. They understand that legal practice evolves, and they must adapt. Lawyers with a growth mindset actively seek opportunities for self-improvement, whether through further education, mentorship, or skill development.

Transitioning from a fixed mindset to a growth mindset is immensely beneficial for new lawyers. Here are some steps to cultivate a growth mindset:

- Don't avoid difficult cases or tasks. Embrace them as opportunities to learn and improve your skills.
- When encountering setbacks, view them as feedback for improvement rather than personal shortcomings.
- Actively seek feedback from mentors, colleagues, and clients. Constructive criticism is invaluable for growth.
- Persistence is key. Continue to develop your skills and knowledge, even when faced with obstacles.
- Prioritise self-care and well-being. A resilient mindset allows you to weather the storms of the legal profession.
- Study successful lawyers and their journeys. Understand that their success was built on dedication, learning, and growth.

In addition, **self-awareness is crucial** because it enables you to do your best by sharpening your strengths and working on your weaknesses.

To illustrate, let's say you have a problem getting to work on time. If you are aware of the problem and the circumstances that lead to it, you can consciously try to find ways to deal with the issues.

Self-awareness helps you set more meaningful goals and make better decisions. This enables you to develop a greater sense of purpose and direction in life.

On the other hand, if you don't know what you like or how you work, you'll find it harder to work since you won't be working at your best. That is why you should figure out your strengths and weaknesses, likes and dislikes, and ideal work environment. Such an environment will support your growth.

By adopting a growth mindset, new lawyers can position themselves for long-term success, personal development, and fulfilment in the dynamic world of law. Remember, your perspective is not set in stone; it's a skill you can develop and refine over time, empowering you to thrive in your legal career.

And when you meet an obstacle, don't be too quick to conclude that there's nothing you can do about it. Instead, ask for help and consider how others deal with similar situations. Sometimes, obstacles seem more significant than they are because you've never dealt with them before. But once you encounter and deal with them, you'll gain the experience to deal with similar situations more calmly.

MANAGING STRESS, BURNOUT AND VICARIOUS TRAUMA

Stress and burnout can hinder career performance and development, complicate personal relationships, and make work-life balance challenging. If you want to develop a strong foundation for your career, you must learn to manage stress and burnout.

Unfortunately, many lawyers fail to seek help even when their firms offer resilience training and counselling services for fear of their bosses and supervisors seeing them as weak.

Some don't even know they're experiencing stress and burnout in the first place! Thus, they go about their workdays feeling physically ill and mentally exhausted without addressing the issue, which negatively impacts their work and home life.

Be alert to the symptoms that can manifest when you are burnt out.

Burnout happens when you feel physically, mentally, and emotionally exhausted due to the prolonged stress and constant demands placed on you.

Its symptoms include:

- Feeling tired and drained.
- Change in appetite.
- Change in sleep habits.
- Lowered immunity and frequent illnesses.
- Frequent headaches.
- Muscle pains.
- Self-doubt.
- Sense of failure.
- Feeling helpless or defeated.
- Loss of motivation.
- Procrastination.
- Drug and alcohol abuse.
- Irritability (that increased level of sass I mentioned in the introduction is usually a good indicator).
- Withdrawing from responsibilities and skipping work.
- Decreased satisfaction in what you do.

When experiencing burnout, getting out of bed becomes a chore, and your work becomes an even bigger chore. You may even notice that you take a very long time to do something you know you can do within no time.

The first step to recovery is knowing what you're suffering from. If you understand the signs of stress and burnout, you can manage them well, which will be critical as you build your career.

Vicarious trauma is the work-related trauma you encounter as you carry out your daily law duties. As a lawyer, you may encounter this type of trauma when you look at videos of exploited people, especially children, when reviewing case files, when clients are recounting their ordeals in the hands of their abusers, or when you witness the aftermath of violence.

While these events happened to someone else, hearing about them and seeing them hurts you because you're a human being. As such, you may:

- Shut down or feel emotionally numb.
- Have difficulty managing your emotions.
- Avoid work and meeting clients.
- Use alcohol and drugs to cope with your feelings.
- Feel a sense of hopelessness.
- Become easily distracted and more prone to accidents.
- Suffer from aches and pains.
- Fall sick frequently.
- Suffer from fatigue and have difficulty sleeping.
- Start withdrawing from others and have relationship problems.
- Become irritable, aggressive, violent, and explosive.
- Impaired judgment.
- Lack of insight – this may lead to professional consequences.

These symptoms indicate that something might be happening to you and that you need support.

They describe your pain; if that pain becomes too much, you may look for another career and give up on becoming a lawyer. As such, you have to do something about them.

So, what can you do?

Emily Nagoski, in her book *Burnout: The Secret to Unlocking the Stress Cycle* introduces the concept of the "stress cycle," which is a critical aspect of managing stress. Stress isn't just about the emotional or mental aspects; it also manifests in our bodies physically. Nagoski emphasises that completing the stress cycle is essential for effectively managing stress.

Nagoski notes when you encounter a stressor (such as a challenging case, tight deadlines, or demanding clients), your body responds by going into a state of heightened alertness, commonly known as the "fight-or-flight" response. To complete the stress cycle, your body must physically discharge this stress energy, often through exercise, deep breathing, or relaxation techniques. If the stress cycle isn't completed, it can accumulate over time, leading to burnout.

Nagoski also introduces the "Human Giver Syndrome" concept, which is particularly relevant in the legal profession. Many lawyers, especially those just starting their careers, often feel the need to be "givers" – constantly helping others while neglecting their own needs. This tendency can lead to chronic stress and burnout.

You may find yourself taking on heavy workloads, overextending yourself to meet client demands, and sacrificing your own well-being. Nagoski's book reminds us that it's crucial to recognise and address this pattern.

Boundaries protect you and give you the clarity you need to serve your client well.

You cannot win cases with emotions alone. You must do your research, gather evidence, and prepare your client. You can only do all that if you can look at things objectively and analyse case information without letting your worries and emotions cloud your judgment.

Boundaries make it easier to manage stress, maintain ethics and professional responsibility and maintain healthy personal and professional relationships.

To set boundaries, you should:

- You need to know your role as a lawyer and avoid playing psychologist or doing work that others can help you do.
- Delegate work instead of trying to do it all. If you cannot do something, learn to say no. Always track all your assignments and how long they will take to complete. This will help you turn down work you cannot do and prioritise your given tasks.
- Schedules help you maintain a healthy work-life balance.
- When you communicate clearly, you leave no room for misunderstandings and let others know your boundaries.
- You do not need to be always available. For example, instead of having your work emails on your phone, you can determine when you'll check your email on a computer.

When you set boundaries, you give yourself enough time to do your work and get some rest, which helps you de-stress and build a strong foundation since you'll have a chance to recharge and find the strength to tackle the next job.

You must learn to **care for your mind, body, and soul**.

Think of activities you can engage in that will relax you. They should be something you love, and that won't set you back as an individual. So, for example, instead of relaxing by drinking alcohol and abusing drugs, you can relax by taking a hot bath and going for a nature walk.

The trick is to find healthy ways to relieve pent-up stress and, as Emily Nagoski notes, "close the stress cycle." A 20-minute walk or yoga session is the perfect reset for me, especially on days when I feel like I don't have the time.

Recognise that stress is both a mental and physical response. Engage in activities that help discharge the physical energy associated with stress, such as regular exercise, deep breathing exercises, or mindfulness meditation.

It helps to **talk to a professional** when in a high-pressure environment. Talking to a professional will help you sort out your emotions so you can have the strength to do your job well and for longer.

Stress and burnout are formidable foes in the legal profession, but with these insights, you can develop effective strategies for managing stress and prioritising your well-being. By understanding the stress cycle, recognising "Human Giver Syndrome," and implementing practical techniques, you can build a thriving legal career while maintaining your physical and mental health. Remember, managing stress is not a sign of weakness; it's a testament to your resilience and commitment to long-term success.

THE GUIDING HAND OF MENTORS (PART 1)

As you embark on your journey into the legal profession, one invaluable asset you should seek early on is a mentor. Mentors are like beacons in the often turbulent seas of legal practice. They are experienced guides who can guide your path, provide wisdom, and share their hard-earned insights.

A mentor can offer more than just technical advice or a window into the intricacies of the law. They can help you navigate the profession's nuances, provide real-world context to legal theory, and teach you the unwritten rules of the legal landscape. They can impart critical skills such as effective client communication, negotiation tactics, and networking, which are vital for a thriving legal career.

Moreover, mentors generally serve as living embodiments of success in the legal world. They've faced the challenges, learned from missteps, and emerged wiser and stronger. By observing and learning from their journeys, you'll gain valuable insights into what it takes to excel in the legal profession. Mentors can help you set realistic career goals, avoid common pitfalls, and identify growth opportunities you might otherwise overlook. Essentially, they become your confidants, allies, and, at times, your most trusted advisors in your legal odyssey.

So, where can you find a mentor to assist?

Attend legal **networking events**, conferences, seminars, and workshops. These gatherings are prime opportunities to meet seasoned professionals who might be open to mentoring. Don't be shy; initiate conversations, express your aspirations, and ask for guidance.

Join **online communities and platforms** dedicated to legal professionals. Websites like LinkedIn and legal forums often host discussions and mentorship opportunities. Follow legal practitioners who are leaders in the field or who inspire you because of how they practice law. Reach out to potential mentors through these platforms.

If you're already employed in a law firm or legal organisation, **ask about mentorship programs within your workplace**. Many firms encourage mentorship to foster professional growth.

Reach out to legal professionals you admire. Send them a respectful and well-crafted message or email expressing your admiration for their work and your interest in potential mentorship. Remember that not everyone will respond, but some may be open to mentoring.

Seek **recommendations** from professors, colleagues, or classmates. They might know someone who would be a suitable mentor based on your specific goals and needs.

Remember that finding the right mentor may take time, and not every mentorship relationship will be a perfect fit. Looking for someone who aligns with your career goals, values, and communication style is crucial. Additionally, be open to reciprocal mentorship, where both parties can learn from each other's experiences and insights.

We'll come back to mentorship in Chapter 6.

BUILDING A SUPPORT NETWORK

A support network is vital to your physical and mental well-being. It is the glue that holds your foundation together.

The high pressure environment of the legal profession can affect your well-being, especially when you're new and don't know the tricks and tips to navigate various situations.

A support network will cheer you on and give you guidance and emotional and professional support.

Think of a support network as a group of people who can lend you a hand in various circumstances. With this in mind, your network can include:

- Your colleagues and peers.
- Family and friends.
- Professional groups and associations.
- Personal therapists or counsellors.

Imagine your journey through the legal profession as a challenging expedition. Now, think about your support network as the team of expert climbers who accompany you, ensuring you easily conquer every peak. As Thurgood Marshall, the iconic civil rights lawyer and the first African-American justice of the Supreme Court, famously said:

"None of us got where we are solely by pulling ourselves up by our bootstraps. We got here because somebody – a parent, a teacher, an Ivy League crony or a few nuns – bent down and helped us pick up our boots."

Consider your family as the reliable base camp for this expedition. When they're part of your support network, they're not just cheering you on from the sidelines; they're the ones preparing hearty meals to fuel your journey and ensuring you find moments of tranquility amidst the chaos. Their unwavering support enables you to nourish your body and soul, even in the throes of your most challenging cases.

However, building a robust support network requires more than simply adding names to a contact list. It hinges on cultivating genuine connections based on mutual respect and reciprocity. Just as you appreciate the warmth of a home-cooked meal, your family members and colleagues crave acknowledgment and appreciation for their contributions.

Imagine a colleague going out of their way to assist you with a project. In return, you reciprocate by offering your support when they need it most. This cycle of kindness and mutual assistance forms the foundation of a strong support network.

So, how do you cultivate such connections? Start by nurturing relationships with those you already know. Leverage networking platforms like LinkedIn to reconnect with former classmates, colleagues, and acquaintances. Simple gestures, like offering a warm greeting and expressing gratitude, can leave a lasting impression, whether you're interacting with the barista who brews your morning coffee or your legal team.

Remember, the friendships you forge early in your legal career are invaluable assets. Embrace the opportunity to network and connect with fellow professionals – it's not just about advancing your career; it's about building a community that uplifts and supports you through every twist and turn of your professional journey. So, take the time to invest in meaningful connections; your future self will thank you for it.

PRACTICAL EXERCISES

Reflection allows us to delve deeper into the material or experience we've encountered. It helps us move beyond surface-level knowledge and comprehension by encouraging critical thinking, analysis, and synthesis of information. We can connect new knowledge to existing knowledge through reflection, making it more meaningful and memorable. With that in mind, here are some practical exercises that you can use to reflect on the themes of Chapter 2:

1. **Mindset Shift:** Identify a specific area where you've encountered challenges or self-doubt in your legal journey. Challenge yourself to adopt a growth mindset by reframing your thoughts. For every negative or fixed belief, replace it with a growth-oriented perspective. Track your progress and note any improvements in your approach.
2. **Stress Coping Strategies:** Create a personal stress coping strategy toolkit. Research and compile various stress-relief techniques such as mindfulness, meditation, physical activities, and breathing exercises. Experiment with these methods and determine which ones work best for you. Having a toolkit of stress management techniques is invaluable in the legal profession.
3. **Expectations Discussion:** Engage in a candid conversation with a practising lawyer, a colleague or someone you might consider as a future mentor about the expectations and realities of the legal profession. Ask them to share their experiences and insights. This firsthand knowledge will provide a practical perspective.

Incorporating regular reflection into our learning and decision-making processes can lead to more meaningful and effective outcomes in our personal and professional lives.

CONCLUSION

In this chapter, we've covered the essential foundations of the profession and ethics (which is cool and powerful) and an understanding of the law firm currency of billable hours. We have also worked through the magic of the right mindset, the importance of mentors, being on the lookout for burnout and building a support network. Phew. A big chapter on foundations. My key points are these:

- When things start to go wrong professionally, it can be a slippery slope, and for that reason, it is helpful to return to the foundations of what it means to be a lawyer and the importance of our fundamental duties.
- Do the right thing, always. Ethical standards are the bedrock upon which the legal profession is built. Lawyers hold a unique position in society, entrusted with the responsibility to advocate for justice and the rule of law. This privilege has a corresponding duty to always uphold the highest ethical standards.
- Burnout happens when you feel physically, mentally, and emotionally exhausted due to the prolonged stress and constant demands placed on you. As a lawyer who has twice meandered down the path to burnout, be alert to the symptoms from the outset and set yourself up for success to avoid it.

What are your key takeaways? Make a note, get a sticky note, highlight, and keep reflecting on how you can incorporate key themes that resonate with you into your daily life.

Ah, work-life balance! That elusive unicorn of adulthood, rumoured to exist but rarely spotted in the wild. We've all heard the legends and tales of mythical creatures who can seamlessly juggle office meetings, family dinners, and yoga classes without breaking a sweat. But let's face it, for most of us, it's as real as a leprechaun riding a unicorn under a rainbow.

In this wondrous world of modern work, we find ourselves on a never-ending quest for the Holy Grail of balance. We try to compartmentalise our lives like ingredients in a meal prep container – one section for work, one for family, one for hobbies, and, of course, one for binge-watching cat videos. But, alas, it seems that these compartments have a peculiar habit of spilling into each other, turning our beautifully organised lives into a pot of spaghetti, with everything tangled together.

And just when you think you've struck the perfect balance, a wild deadline appears, or your kid's science project turns into a volcanic eruption in the middle of your living room. Suddenly, your quest for balance feels more like a quest for survival.

So, here's a thought: what if the secret to work-life balance is realising that it's a bit like hunting for Bigfoot? It's a fantastic tale that's fun to chase but doesn't really exist. Maybe, just maybe, instead of balance, we should aim for harmony – the art of going with the flow, accepting the messiness of life, and occasionally laughing at the absurdity of it all.

After all, in a world where meetings can happen in pyjama bottoms and our to-do lists multiply like rabbits, isn't embracing the chaos part of the adventure?

UNLOCKING THE SECRETS OF WORK-LIFE HARMONY

Picture this: You're at a crossroads, and on one path lies the glowing sign of "Work," and on the other, "Life." But, as it turns out, it's not so much a choice between two paths as it is a precarious balancing act on a tightrope – challenging, often amusing, and occasionally a little bit dangerous.

Your work and life are like dance partners in a never-ending tango. When you've been cha-cha-cha-ing at your desk for hours, your body might just decide to rumba with aches and pains. And when the music stops, you're too exhausted to salsa your way through an evening yoga class. **It's a choreographed drama of body and mind, and finding harmony is the key**.

In this intricate dance, **your personal relationships are like the rhythm section – they set the beat for your life**. A tough day at work can make your foot stumble on the relationship dance floor, leading to a discordant evening. Conversely, the strains of your personal life can echo into your professional world. It's a delicate balance that, when misjudged, can turn your social waltz into a chaotic breakdance.

Imagine you're in an office where the lights never dim, and the coffee machine never rests. While your dedication may be commendable, it could send a different message – that you're working longer, not smarter. It's not a good look for your professional reputation. **Balancing your work and life is like fine-tuning an instrument; it's about making each note count, not playing the longest solo**.

Finally, there's productivity, the syncopated beat of your professional life. It's not about filling every minute with work but making every minute count. **A lack of balance can lead to poor time management and a drop in the quality of your work**. After all, your duty as a lawyer is to help the Court and your clients effectively. If you're drowning in work, you might need a lifeline to stay afloat.

In this grand performance called life, work-life balance is the magical act of keeping all your plates spinning without letting one crash to the ground. It's a dance, a symphony, a balancing act, and a masterpiece in the making. The secret? It's not about choosing one over the other; **it's about finding the rhythm that allows you to enjoy both**.

THE PERILS OF AN UNBALANCED LIFE

Imagine your life as a delicate ecosystem where work and personal well-being must coexist in harmony. When this equilibrium is disrupted, like throwing a pebble into a still pond, the ripples of imbalance can lead to a series of unforeseen consequences.

First up, let's talk about your well-being. **An imbalanced life can have your body and mind crying out for help**. Imagine a crescendo of stress-induced insomnia, digestive troubles, pounding headaches, and the ominous shadow of cardiovascular issues. It's like the sinister background music of a thriller movie, signalling impending danger.

Next on our list is the notorious burnout, the ultimate nemesis of every overworked individual. **Burnout doesn't knock politely; it barges in with physical, mental, and emotional exhaustion**. It's your body's way of raising the white flag, shouting, "Enough is enough!" It's like a stern parent sending you to a time-out when you refuse to take a break yourself.

Now, picture your relationships. They are symphonies of life, but **when your every note is about work, the melody can start to sound rather monotonous**. Friends and family may feel like mere spectators in your life, always waiting for you to finish your solo and join the ensemble. Relationships strain, and the music grows discordant.

In the circus of life, **long hours don't make you the star performer; they turn you into a clumsy juggler dropping balls left and right**. Productivity takes a nosedive as your concentration wavers, and you start making decisions that would make a clown blush.

Lastly, there's **the cruel irony of overworking – reduced job satisfaction**. When you dedicate every waking moment to work, success is the expectation, not the exception; the spotlight only shines when you falter. It's like receiving applause when you lose, not when you win. The allure of the stage dims, and the standing ovations grow scarce.

In this grand opera of life, failing to strike the right chord in the delicate balance between work and well-being can lead to a cacophony of chaos. It's a warning siren, a neon sign flashing "Danger," and a call to action. So, take a moment, reevaluate your life's orchestration, and find the sweet harmony waiting to be discovered.

UNLOCKING THE SECRETS OF A BALANCED LIFE

Close your eyes for a moment and imagine this: a life where work is not a relentless race but a rhythmic dance, where the symphony of your ambitions harmonises with the melody of your personal well-being. It sounds like a myth, doesn't it? Well, it's not. Achieving a healthy work-life balance is not a far-fetched dream; it's an attainable reality, and here's how you can make it happen.

Look after your body.

Let's start with your body, the temple of your existence. It's your vessel for pursuing dreams and cherishing moments. Neglecting it is like driving a car without ever changing the oil. Sure, it works for a while, but eventually, it sputters and stalls.

Consider this: you're a lawyer with dreams and ambitions, but your body is your vehicle to reach those goals. How far can you go on an empty tank or with a sluggish engine? Not very far.

Now, think of regular exercise, wholesome meals, and adequate rest as the fuel, the oil change, and the tune-up your body needs.

These investments give you the strength and stamina to tackle work challenges and family life's joys. You're sharpening your knife for efficient cutting, not struggling with a blunt instrument.

Remember Emily Nagoski's advice on Burnout in Chapter 2 – you need to "close the stress cycle." Incorporate mindfulness practices into your daily routine. Activities like meditation, deep breathing exercises, or yoga can help you stay grounded and reduce stress. Regular exercise has a profound impact on reducing stress and improving mood. Find an activity you enjoy and make it a part of your routine.

By prioritising your physical well-being, you'll move through life gracefully and efficiently, cutting through obstacles and achieving your goals while still having the energy to enjoy the journey.

Look after your mind.

Your mind is a garden, and like any garden, it needs tending. As you embark on your legal career, you'll encounter the thorns and brambles of a challenging profession. You may wonder how some people can be so unkind, and you'll face situations where you're powerless to help. It's like navigating a maze of frustration and disillusionment.

This is where mental health self-care becomes your compass. Picture meditation and mindfulness as the oases in this legal desert. Meditation is the calming sanctuary where your mind can rest, away from the relentless world. It's where you observe without judgment, like watching a flickering candle flame.

Mindfulness keeps you grounded in the present moment, helping you focus and excel in your work. It's your secret weapon against the distractions that lurk around every corner of your mind.

But what about when you need a guide to help you navigate the maze of your thoughts and emotions? That's where therapy comes in. **Therapy is your wise mentor, helping you sift through the tangled**

underbrush of your mind and emotions. It teaches you the art of acceptance and the power of letting go.

So, whether it's meditation's serenity, mindfulness's focus, or therapy's guidance, looking after your mental well-being is essential to manage what can sometimes be turbulent times in legal practice.

Look after your spirit.

Now, let's talk about nurturing your spirit, the intangible force that adds depth and purpose to your life. It's about finding meaning beyond your day-to-day aspirations, like discovering hidden treasures beneath the surface.

Some seek spiritual nourishment through religious practices, while others find it in creative endeavours or the embrace of nature. It's about connecting to something larger than yourself and realising that life extends beyond your ambitions.

Imagine spending time studying nature, humbled by the vastness of what you don't know. This newfound humility translates into patience and understanding when dealing with others. It's a reminder that there's more to life than meets the eye.

Nurturing your spirit is about finding balance not just between work and life but between your ambitions and your inner self.

So, as you embark on this journey towards a balanced life, remember: it's not about splitting your time in half but about finding harmony in the different notes of your existence.

BREAKING THE CHAINS OF OVERWORK: A BLUEPRINT FOR BALANCE

Now, let's tackle some practical steps to reclaim your life from the jaws of overwork.

Picture this: you, diligently perched at your desk day in and day out, yearning for that one big case that will catapult you to stardom in the legal world. While ambition is admirable, an overdose of it can rob you of life's simple pleasures.

Fear of Missing Out (FOMO) is common among lawyers, especially those starting their careers. The allure of high-profile cases can be magnetic, but if you find yourself sacrificing your life outside the office on the altar of ambition, it's time to hit the brakes.

Remember, you're not just a lawyer but a human being. **It's okay to strive for greatness, but not at the cost of your well-being and personal life**. Cherish the moments with loved ones, enjoy leisurely lunches, and regain your work-life equilibrium.

New lawyers often feel the weight of the world on their shoulders, believing they must prove their worth by taking on a Herculean workload. The myth that overworking is the only path to success can lead to burnout faster than you can say "legal brief." Remember, Emily Nagoski calls this the "Human Giver Syndrome."

Sure, impressing your superiors is important, but not at the expense of your health and sanity. Understand that quality often trumps quantity. Working smart, not just hard, is the name of the game.

Overworking doesn't equate to better results; it often results in exhaustion, health issues, and diminishing returns. Instead, focus on efficiency, prioritise self-care, and watch your productivity soar.

Disorganisation can be the nemesis of work-life balance. **Invest time structuring your tasks, setting priorities, and maintaining an organised workspace**. A clutter-free desk is like a clear highway for productivity.

Remember, your ultimate goal as a lawyer should be to serve your clients effectively, not merely to rack up billable hours. By focusing on delivering value rather than hours worked, you'll free up precious time for yourself.

While organisation is vital, avoid micromanaging your time. Allow room for spontaneity within your schedule. Designate time for yourself daily, but leave the activities flexible. This way, you can decide on the spot whether to indulge in a yoga session, a jog or a walk around the park.

It's not just about doing less; it's about doing what truly matters. Investing in yourself is the key to a successful career and a fulfilling life. Identify areas for improvement, whether it's a healthier diet, less caffeine, regular exercise, or nurturing your mental health.

In today's hyper-connected world, interruptions are lurking around every digital corner. At the office, resist the temptation to engage in non-urgent phone calls or prolonged water-cooler conversations. **Set clear boundaries for your work time to minimise interruptions**.

Similarly, when you leave the office, **mentally detach from work**. Silence those email notifications, resist checking your work phone, and allow yourself the mental space to recharge.

Dr Adam Fraser has a great book on balancing work and life. *The Third Space* discusses the importance of effectively transitioning between different aspects of life to find balance, fulfilment, and happiness.

Dr Fraser identifies three critical spaces in our daily lives:

1. **The First Space:** This represents our work or professional life. It includes all the tasks, responsibilities, and challenges associated with our career.
2. **The Second Space:** The second space is our personal life, encompassing family, friends, hobbies, and personal well-being. It's where we seek relaxation, joy, and fulfilment outside of work.
3. **The Third Space:** The third space is the transitional zone between the first and second spaces. It's the critical space where

we switch our focus from work to personal life and vice versa. Effectively transitioning through the third space is essential for maintaining a healthy work-life balance.

The third space is where we reset our minds and emotions. Dr Fraser says it is the buffer zone that allows us to leave the stresses of work behind and fully engage in our personal lives and vice versa. Getting the transition right is crucial to reducing stress, maintaining relationships, and enhancing productivity.

So how can we do that? We have already talked a lot about **boundaries**, so you know their importance by now.

Establish **transition rituals** that signal your brain it's time to shift from one space to another. These can include a short walk, deep breathing, or simply taking a moment to reflect. Sometimes, it can be the drive or train ride home listening to your favourite music or audiobook.

Schedule short breaks between work and personal activities to give yourself time to transition effectively. Incorporate **mindfulness** and relaxation techniques to help you stay present in each space.

Communicate your boundaries and needs to your colleagues and loved ones so they understand and respect your transition times.

Mastering the third space is crucial. Legal practice often involves high-pressure situations, long hours, and tight deadlines. Learning to transition effectively between work and personal life can help you maintain your well-being, nurture relationships, and find balance and happiness in both your careers and personal lives.

Ask for help

While this book provides several self-help strategies and techniques, sometimes it's essential to recognise that seeking professional support is a vital and necessary step on the path to recovery and resilience.

In her book *Burnout*, Emily Nagoski emphasises the critical role of therapy and counselling in addressing burnout and vicarious trauma. Those comments are also relevant to caring for our general mental health. Here's why seeking professional support is often the wisest choice.

Therapists and counsellors provide an **objective and non-judgmental perspective**. They are trained to listen, understand, and help you navigate complex emotions and experiences without bias.

Mental health professionals have **specialised knowledge and techniques** to address burnout, vicarious trauma, and related mental health issues. They can tailor their approach to your needs, ensuring you receive effective support.

Therapy and counselling sessions offer **a safe and confidential space to express your thoughts and feelings**. This can be especially valuable when dealing with the emotional toll of legal practice, where privacy and trust are paramount.

Professionals can **teach you coping strategies and resilience-building techniques tailored to your specific challenges**. These strategies empower you to manage stress and prevent burnout.

Early intervention through therapy or counselling **can prevent stress and burnout from escalating into more severe mental health issues**. It's a proactive step toward safeguarding your well-being.

Signs You Might Benefit from Therapy

Recognising when to seek therapy or counselling is crucial to self-care. Some signs that treatment could be beneficial include:

- Persistent feelings of emotional exhaustion or hopelessness.
- Difficulty managing stress, anxiety, or depression.
- Intrusive thoughts related to traumatic experiences.

- A decline in the quality of your personal and professional life.
- Struggles with maintaining healthy boundaries.

Overcoming Stigma

In law, as in many other professions, there has been a long-standing stigma surrounding mental health and seeking therapy or counselling. This stigma often arises from misconceptions and societal pressures that discourage individuals from openly addressing their mental health needs. However, it's essential to challenge and overcome this stigma for the well-being of legal practitioners.

One of the most pervasive myths is that **seeking therapy signifies weakness** or an inability to cope with life's challenges independently. In reality, therapy is a proactive and courageous step toward self-improvement and emotional well-being.

There's often **a fear that colleagues, employers, or clients will judge legal professionals who seek therapy**. This fear can lead to reluctance to seek help, even when desperately needed. It's important to remember that mental health support is a personal decision, and confidentiality is a fundamental aspect of therapy.

Some individuals worry that acknowledging mental health struggles may **negatively impact their professional reputation**. However, the profession is evolving, recognising the importance of mental health, and many bar and law associations now promote well-being as a core value.

The Importance of Challenging Stigma

Overcoming the stigma of seeking therapy or counselling is essential.

When the stigma is reduced, legal professionals are more likely to seek help when experiencing burnout, vicarious trauma, or other mental health challenges. We **promote early intervention and better**

mental health outcomes by fostering an environment that supports help-seeking behaviour.

Mental health support is a crucial component of overall well-being. By embracing therapy and counselling as valuable resources, lawyers can **improve their mental health, enhance resilience, and ultimately perform better in their roles**.

Open discussions about mental health and therapy help **create a supportive legal community**. When colleagues share their experiences and normalise seeking help, it encourages others to do the same. This sense of community reduces isolation and strengthens the profession.

Overcoming the stigma surrounding therapy and counselling is a collective effort. By challenging misconceptions, fostering open conversations, and advocating for change, the legal profession can create an environment where mental health support is accepted and encouraged. This shift is vital for the well-being of legal professionals and the continued evolution of a healthier, more compassionate legal community. Remember, seeking therapy is a courageous step toward a more balanced and fulfilling legal career.

SELF-CARE CHECKLIST

When we reflect on what we've learned, we reinforce our memory of the material. This cognitive rehearsal helps consolidate new information into long-term memory, making it more likely that we will remember and be able to apply what we've learned in the future. With that in mind, here is a self-care checklist that you can use to reflect on the themes of Chapter 3:

1. **Self-reflection:** Set aside time for regular self-reflection. Assess your current work-life balance and identify areas that require improvement.

2. **Establish boundaries:** Define clear boundaries between work and personal life. Do not check work emails or engage in work-related tasks during your designated personal time.
3. **Prioritise time blocks:** Implement time-blocking techniques to allocate dedicated time for work, personal life, and leisure activities. Stick to these time blocks as closely as possible.
4. **Delegate tasks:** When possible, delegate tasks and responsibilities at work. Empower your team members or support staff to take on specific tasks, reducing your workload.
5. **Use technology mindfully:** Embrace technology to enhance efficiency, but use it mindfully. Avoid unnecessary screen time during personal hours and consider digital detox periods.
6. **Quality over quantity:** Focus on the quality of your work rather than the quantity of hours spent working. Efficiency and effectiveness often lead to a healthier work-life balance.
7. **Regular breaks:** Incorporate regular breaks into your workday to recharge. Short, frequent breaks can boost productivity and reduce stress.
8. **Wellness activities:** Engage in wellness activities such as exercise, meditation, or mindfulness to maintain physical and mental health.
9. **Social connections:** Foster and prioritise social connections with friends and family. Allocate time for socialising to strengthen personal relationships.
10. **Unplug:** Designate specific periods or days for a digital detox. Disconnect from screens and engage in analog activities that bring joy and relaxation.
11. **Set realistic goals:** Set achievable goals and manage your workload realistically. Avoid overcommitting to tasks and projects.

12. **Learn to say "no":** Practice saying "no" when your plate is full. Prioritise your existing commitments and decline additional responsibilities if necessary.
13. **Evaluate time wasters:** Identify and eliminate time-wasting habits or activities that offer little value to your personal or professional life.
14. **Regular evaluation:** Periodically review and adjust your work-life balance strategies. Be flexible and willing to adapt to changing circumstances.
15. **Seek support:** Don't hesitate to seek support from mentors, coaches, or counsellors if you're struggling to achieve balance or facing burnout.
16. **Celebrate achievements:** Acknowledge your achievements, both big and small, and take pride in your work.
17. **Set personal goals:** Define personal goals and aspirations outside of your legal career. Allocate time and effort toward pursuing these goals.
18. **Work-life harmony:** Embrace the concept of work-life harmony, where aspects of your personal life can complement and coexist with your professional life.
19. **Time for hobbies:** Rekindle or develop hobbies and interests that bring joy and fulfilment. Dedicate time to pursue these passions.
20. **Mindful self-care:** Practice mindful self-care by listening to your physical and emotional needs. Be kind to yourself and prioritise your well-being.

Remember that prioritising your well-being benefits you personally and enhances your effectiveness and longevity in your legal career.

CONCLUSION

In this chapter, we've covered the importance of understanding and implementing work-life balance, and if not, then, at the very least, harmony. Boundaries are a key driver in helping you do that. We have also worked through the importance of looking after your body, mind and spirit and asking for help when things feel overwhelming. Dr Fraser's takeaways from "The Third Space" provide immediate practical tools to transition between work and life. My key points are these:

- Your mind is your most important asset as a lawyer; without it, you cannot effectively do your job. It requires rest, exercise, and mindfulness. Look after it well.
- Find something that nurtures your spirit beyond the law. The thing that lights you up when to do it or talk about it. Do that, a lot.
- Work out your transition space and transition rituals. My music played (mostly loudly) in the car on my way home is a total reset between work and home. Find your thing.

What are your key takeaways? Make a note, get a sticky note, highlight, and keep reflecting on how you can incorporate key themes that resonate with you into your daily life.

Chapter 4:

This is how we do things here

As you step into the hallowed halls of a law firm, you're entering a world not entirely dissimilar from a children's playgroup. Curious, isn't it? Think back to those playground days when you were a child. Remember how effortlessly you approached others, forming friendships within moments and gleefully diving into shared adventures? Children are masters of spontaneous connection.

Yet, as adults, our approach to working and interacting with others often takes a more measured tone. We've learned, through experience, the perils of indiscriminate interaction and the complexities that come with it. Our interactions are marked by a deliberate caution, a recognition of the nuances and intricacies of social dynamics.

However, this cautious approach, while sensible, doesn't negate the essence of connection. It underscores the importance of it. You're no longer on the playground, but the skills you've honed in your early social experiences will serve you remarkably well as you embark on your legal career.

In the legal profession, you will collaborate with individuals from various walks of life, each contributing their unique perspective and expertise. Learning to navigate this intricate web of relationships is a vital skill that will ease your day-to-day life at the law firm and bolster your journey towards becoming a thriving lawyer.

Ultimately, your goal is clear: to thrive as a lawyer. Every action you take, every interaction you engage in, should be a strategic step toward making your daily life at the law firm more manageable.

Remember that your legal career is not a solitary but a collaborative endeavour. By mastering the skills and insights shared here, you will thrive within the law firm's bustling ecosystem and harmonise your unique skills into a resounding success story.

LEARN THE CULTURE OF YOUR LAW FIRM

As you step into the world of lawyering, it's crucial to grasp a fundamental truth: no two law firms are the same. It's like entering a grand ensemble, where each firm plays its distinct tune, composed of written and unwritten rules that guide their daily symphony. Whether you're contemplating a small sole practitioner's firm or a bustling international giant, every firm has its own rhythm and unique culture.

People with diverse backgrounds and experiences converge within these legal spaces, crafting their own narratives of norms and values. They expect newcomers to dance to the same beat. This is where the concept of a law firm's culture takes centre stage, and understanding it can be the key to deciding if this is the stage you want to grace with your legal expertise.

In her book *Just Work*, Kim Scott provides valuable insights into fostering a healthy workplace culture and effectively addressing workplace issues. Organisational culture is the invisible force that shapes behaviour, decisions, and interactions within a law firm.

So, what aspects of this legal culture should you be attuned to? Consider the following as your checklist:

- **Core values and norms:** Every firm has its guiding principles, the moral compass that points to its legal endeavours. Scott says it is essential to familiarise yourself with your firm's stated values and mission. Understanding these core principles can guide your actions and decisions.
- **Communication norms:** The way information flows, the tone of discussions, and the importance of clear communication are pivotal.
- **Time and output expectations:** Is it a firm that thrives on a nine-to-five routine, or does it embrace flexibility and expect results above all?

- **Career development opportunities:** Are there paths for growth, mentorship programs, and opportunities to elevate your legal prowess?
- **Social connections:** The camaraderie between colleagues can significantly impact your work life.
- **Approach to decision making:** Is it a hierarchical structure, or do they encourage collaborative decision-making?
- **Bonuses and incentives:** The financial incentives and recognition for your hard work matter.
- **Flex-time programs:** Does the firm offer flexibility to accommodate your personal needs?

Immerse yourself in the firm's culture, scrutinise its norms, and ask yourself, "Is this where I want to be?" If the answer is a resounding yes, adapt and grow within its hallways. However, if you feel like an outsider, unable to access the resources and support needed for your success, it may be time to consider alternative arrangements.

If you are still unsure, then ask this question: Does this firm make me proud? Your workplace should be a source of inspiration, not an anchor of shame or sadness. Many lawyers, driven by dreams of promotions or partnerships, endure years in a joyless work environment. But you don't have to be one of them.

If your current legal habitat feels like a cage, it's time to reflect on your aspirations and what you're willing to endure for the sake of your career. Don't let the relentless pursuit of a title blind you to the importance of your well-being and fulfilment.

Lastly, a word about the darker side of some legal cultures. Some firms, in a misguided attempt at 'welcoming,' subject new colleagues to unsavoury assignments and even bullying. Some managers are great lawyers but not great leaders, resorting to threats, intimidation, and aggression. If you find yourself in such an atmosphere, you're not alone. The legal profession has lost too many bright stars to this behaviour. Scott says it is crucial to address workplace issues promptly and effectively. If you encounter an issue that affects your work or ethics, address it directly with the involved parties. Avoiding conflicts only perpetuates the problem.

As you navigate these challenges, remember that you can shape the culture around you. Stand up against bullying, support your peers, and be a beacon of change. Together, we can foster a legal world where every lawyer thrives in a profession of respect and camaraderie.

BUILD RELATIONSHIPS WITH COLLEAGUES

You will spend considerable time with your colleagues, so building a good relationship with them makes sense.

You can do that if you do things like:

- Be friendly and approachable to others without encroaching on their boundaries or allowing them to disrespect yours.
- Look for opportunities to collaborate with your colleagues. Doing this will allow you to get to know each other and form stronger bonds. Also, don't belittle others because they are the support staff. You need different people to get your job done.
- Don't blurt out things someone said to you in confidence, and avoid gossiping about other colleagues. If you have a question about a colleague, ask the colleague instead of asking others or making assumptions.
- Your colleagues don't need to know every detail of your life, so avoid oversharing. That's a sure way to make them uncomfortable.
- Instead of shunning others because they're different from you,

embrace diversity and the innovation and creativity diverse people bring to the workplace.
- When invited to an event, try to arrive early and leave later to get more opportunities to interact with the people there. But don't try to do to take over the events. Instead, listen as others talk. Engage in conversation instead of focusing on yourself.

If you can build a good relationship with your colleagues, you'll find it easier to work with them, and your work will be easier.

EMBRACE TIME MANAGEMENT AND PRODUCTIVITY

From the moment you step into the world of law firms, the clock becomes your constant companion. Being a lawyer is not just about mastering the intricacies of legal doctrine; it's also about conquering the relentless passage of time. Every day you will need to deftly juggle multiple roles and tasks.

If you let time slip through your fingers like grains of sand, you'll find it challenging work effectively. The career ladder may remain just out of reach, and your legal journey might not flow as you had hoped it might.

On the flip side, by honing your time management skills, you'll become a maestro of productivity. Your days will unfold like a carefully crafted masterpiece, guided by your adeptness. In this coordination, you'll not only fulfil client needs but surpass them as administrative duties streamline, granting you the freedom to prioritize essential tasks.

Carefully harnessed, your time will be an ally in your pursuit of excellence. It will fuel your professional development, keeping you attuned to the ever-evolving legal landscape. You'll meet and exceed your firm's expectations and initiatives, setting a pace that others can only aspire to match.

Yet, amidst the relentless pace of legal life, don't forget to reserve space for yourself. Self-care is not a luxury but a necessity for sustaining your brilliance. The pause between notes gives music its soul; likewise, self-care enriches your legal journey.

Above all, remember that the legal career is a marathon, not a sprint. To maintain the cadence of excellence, you must cultivate a healthy work-life balance.

So, how can you manage your time well and increase productivity?

First and foremost, **work smarter, not harder**.

Look at all the tasks you do in a day and determine where you can improve your workflow. For instance, you can delegate some tasks and have your administrative team tackle the jobs you don't need to do personally.

Always let the client know what you can do and by when.

You'll only hurt your reputation and frustrate your clients, if you over-promise or give yourself less time to complete a task. You'll find yourself working on several tasks that need immediate attention, and guess what: doing this will make it harder to do any of these tasks well.

Distractions steal and eat into your time. If you spend time scrolling and answering your phone, you'll discover you've wasted a lot of time by the end of the day. When you start a task, **mute all notifications until you complete your job**. This includes phone calls, message, and email notifications, and pop-ups.

Complex tasks need your attention and often consume more time than you anticipated. Instead of pushing them aside, it would be better to **complete complex tasks first** and then do the other tasks. Remember – "eat that frog!"

As you become better at estimating the time it will take to do specific tasks, you can find ways to stack certain tasks to give you more time to work on the complex tasks.

Also, remember that some tasks appear complex because you haven't found ways to simplify them. For instance, if you're not used to doing research, you may spend a lot of time on research. But if you know which tools to use, the task may take only a few minutes. So, look for easier ways to do things and automate any tasks you can automate.

Your schedule should not be too strict because being a lawyer means you'll inevitably deal with unforeseen circumstances. If you **leave room in your schedule**, you'll comfortably handle any emergency without interfering with your other jobs too much.

All in all, remember time is an asset, not an enemy. You can use it wisely and endeavour to distribute your tasks well to increase your productivity.

HANDLING FEEDBACK AND CRITICISM

Feedback is integral to personal and professional growth, especially in the legal field. How you handle feedback and criticism will determine how far you grow as a lawyer.

The first thing you need to do is **learn to recognise feedback and understand its importance**.

In *Thanks for the Feedback*, authors Douglas Stone and Sheila Heen provide valuable insights into receiving and using feedback effectively. Stone and Heen identify three primary triggers that affect our reactions to feedback:

1. **Truth triggers:** These relate to the accuracy of the feedback. Do we agree with the validity and fairness of the feedback?
2. **Relationship triggers:** These are linked to the dynamics between the giver and receiver of feedback. How does the relationship influence our response?

3. **Identity triggers:** These involve how feedback impacts our self-worth and identity. Does the feedback challenge our self-concept?

Understanding these triggers is crucial for new lawyers. When feedback comes your way, you must recognise your immediate reactions and what might be triggering them.

One of the core messages in "Thanks for the Feedback" is that feedback is a gift, not a threat. This mindset shift can empower new lawyers to embrace feedback and turn it into an opportunity for growth.

Unfortunately, the people who provide feedback do not usually do it well. Instead, they lash out, shout, lecture, and use words meant to convey their disappointment and disgust. If you focus on their words, tone, and actions, you will fail to hear the message they want to communicate.

So, instead of reacting when someone criticises you, listen to their input, take notes, and then reflect on what they've said. "Thanks for the Feedback" highlights the importance of engaging in productive dialogues to maximise the benefits of feedback.

1. **Active listening:** Pay close attention to the feedback giver's perspective. Show that you value their input.
2. **Ask clarifying questions:** Ask questions that clarify the specific areas or behaviours in question to help you better understand the feedback.
3. **Express gratitude:** Regardless of the feedback's content, express gratitude to the giver for taking the time to provide input.

If you're bothered by the delivery of the feedback, try to speak to the person when they are calm and ask for constructive feedback. This way, the person will tell you what you need to work on instead of telling you you've done an awful job.

Some people are more prone to giving feedback than others, and others don't feel it is their place to provide feedback. Thus, if you are eager to know how you're doing as a lawyer, **you should deliberately ask for feedback**.

When asking for feedback, be specific. Let the person know what you'd like input on instead of asking for feedback in general. This is important because people tend to cut you slack when you're new. They don't mention the little things because they expect you'll become better at doing things as you gain more experience. But when you ask people to comment on a particular thing, they'll feel comfortable telling you things they wouldn't have if they were to speak generally.

Once you ask for feedback, **be ready to listen to it even if you don't like what you hear**. Don't argue with the person giving the feedback, and once someone shares their take, thank them for the feedback. You can also ask them if there is something you can do to work more efficiently.

The idea is to determine the areas you need to work on and note any suggestions that may make you a better lawyer. Since you'll collaborate with various people, you can ask different people for feedback.

The feedback you get is supposed to help you navigate the law firm life. That means you need to use it to improve your work life. It can only do that if you take the time to **evaluate it and make the necessary changes**.

Feedback and criticism are invaluable tools for personal and professional growth in the legal field. Applying these principles allows you to transform feedback into a catalyst for improvement. Embrace feedback as a gift, disentangle its triggers, and engage in constructive feedback conversations to refine your legal skills and excel in your legal career. Remember that feedback is not just about becoming a better lawyer; it's about becoming the best version of yourself in the legal profession.

CELEBRATE ACHIEVEMENTS

Embarking on a legal career is like stepping into a whirlwind of stimuli. It's an arena where theory meets reality; you grapple with real-life cases and confront the consequences of your actions. Amid this relentless rush, it's all too easy to become a legal nomad, drifting from one case to the next without pausing to reflect on your journey.

You tread a dangerous path when you neglect to pause and acknowledge your accomplishments. The road leads to a destination marked by disillusionment, burnout, stress, and unrelenting frustration, especially when the fierce winds of adversity blow your way.

Instead, **embrace the power of celebration**. It's not just a fleeting indulgence; it's a strategic move that can invigorate your legal career. When you celebrate your achievements, you are doing more than just patting yourself on the back; you're infusing your journey with essential fuel.

Here's why celebrating matters:

- Each celebration is a badge of honour, a validation, a testament to your relentless hard work. It's saying, "I did this, and I did it well."
- Celebrations serve as signposts on your path, motivating you to keep marching forward. They're the wind in your sails, propelling you toward more significant accomplishments.
- Achievements celebrated are confidence earned. They're tangible proof of your capabilities, moments to remind yourself that you can achieve your goals.
- Celebrations lock moments in your memory, serving as beacons of positivity during the darkest days. Remembering all that you have achieved will guide you through adversity.
- Celebrations build resilience and remind you that your work

is meaningful and impactful, even when it feels like an uphill battle.

- Burnout finds no sanctuary where achievements are celebrated. They serve as constant reminders that your work has purpose and value.

Celebrating your achievements is a self-empowerment ritual that nurtures the flame of motivation and encouragement. **It reminds you that your work matters** and that, despite the trials and tribulations, success is not just a distant dream – it's a tangible reality within your grasp.

So, as you journey through the legal landscape, remember to pause, applaud your accomplishments, and take a moment to celebrate yourself. In doing so, you'll find the strength to endure and the fortitude to thrive on your path toward a long and fruitful legal career.

PRACTICAL EXERCISES

Reflective learners tend to be more self-directed in their learning journey. They take ownership of their education by setting goals, seeking feedback, and adjusting their approach based on their reflections. This proactive approach fosters a sense of responsibility and autonomy in learning. With that in mind, here are some practical exercises that you can use to reflect on the themes of Chapter 4:

1. **Culture Decoder**: Create a culture decoder document for your law firm. Observe and note the critical aspects of your firm's culture, such as work hours, dress code, communication style, and values. Use this decoder as a reference to adapt effectively to your firm's environment.

2. **Coffee Connections**: Initiate coffee or lunch meetings with colleagues from different departments or levels within your firm. These informal discussions help you understand their roles, share insights, and build valuable relationships outside your immediate team.
3. **Self-Celebration Ritual**: Establish a self-celebration ritual for small and significant achievements. It could be treating yourself to a favourite snack, taking a short break, or practising gratitude. Celebrating your wins, no matter how small, fosters a positive mindset.

Incorporating regular reflection into our learning and decision-making processes can lead to more meaningful and effective outcomes in our personal and professional lives.

CONCLUSION

In this chapter, we've covered understanding your law firm culture, the need to build relationships with your colleagues, and managing your time well. We have also worked through asking for feedback and receiving that well to grow in our legal practice. For me, the most important is the need to stop and celebrate your achievements. In the busy, busy world of law, it's too easy to say, "Oh, that's cool, what's next?" without pausing to impact just how cool it was. My key takeaways are these:

- Understanding "how we do things here" is critical. Knowing what to expect and how to fit in at your new firm will guide how you practice law. Make sure you are across the core values and norms. If you are not sure – ask someone.
- Feedback is always difficult, especially when the person giving it

isn't skilled in communication or doesn't understand the impact of their words. The best you can do is control how you receive feedback and, in particular, understand different triggers that may impact how you hear something. When feedback comes your way, you must recognise your immediate reactions and what might be triggering them.

- I'm guilty of this – big time. I have achieved some great things in my career, and it's easy to tick that off the list and say, "What's next?". Celebrating your achievements reminds you that your work matters, that success is not a distant dream but a tangible reality within your grasp.

What are your key takeaways? Make a note, get a sticky note, highlight, and keep reflecting on how you can incorporate key themes that resonate with you into your daily life.

Chapter 5:

Words Matter: The Power of Effective Communication

Communication is the thread that binds cases, clients, and careers. **With the right words, you can tip the scales of justice, orchestrate settlements, and champion the cause of righteousness**. The skill of articulating ideas with precision and persuasion is not a mere accessory but an indispensable tool that can chart the trajectory of your legal journey.

However, it's not just about courtroom theatrics or dazzling speeches. Effective communication extends far beyond the confines of the courtroom, permeating every aspect of legal practice. It's the bridge that connects you to your clients, colleagues, and the broader professional community.

You don't need to be a born orator to master the art of communication. **You need a keen awareness of the impact your words can have and a commitment to wielding them with care**.

Your role as an advocate extends beyond the courtroom. Your clients turn to you for guidance and solutions because you possess the legal knowledge they lack. Even if you're just starting your legal career, remember that you are better equipped to advocate for your client's cause.

To excel, you must channel your legal acumen effectively. Dive into the case, gather the necessary information, explore viable options, and then impart your advice with clarity and insight. By doing so, you fulfil your duty and foster trust and confidence.

Yet, the influence of communication doesn't stop there. In the legal world, collaboration is paramount. You'll navigate a network of individuals – your team, assistants, managers, bosses, and opposing counsel – all essential components of your legal endeavours. Effective communication emerges as the linchpin that ensures the swift flow of information in a profession where time is often of the essence.

Your communication skills are more than tools; they reflect your professionalism and reputation. The effort you invest in refining these skills will shape how you're perceived within the legal community. By maintaining a commitment to clear, respectful, and ethical communication, you demonstrate your dedication to the profession's standards.

Be mindful that in day-to-day legal practice, **every word you utter can reshape narratives, influence outcomes, and leave an indelible mark**. Communicate with that thought at the forefront of your mind, always.

THE ART OF SILENCE: LISTENING AS A CORNERSTONE OF COMMUNICATION

In a world often abuzz with the ceaseless hum of voices and opinions, paradoxically, the importance of silence cannot be overstated, especially when it comes to effective communication within the legal profession. As we explore the power of words and the nuances of conversation, it's essential to remember that sometimes, the most eloquent communicators are those who say nothing at all.

Listening, as a cornerstone of communication, isn't just about hearing words; it's about understanding the essence behind them. This skill becomes a potent tool in your arsenal. Here's why:

- When you listen actively, you convey to your clients, colleagues, and adversaries that their words hold weight. It's **a gesture of respect, an acknowledgment of their concerns, and a bridge to empathy**. This connection can be invaluable in the often emotionally charged landscape of law.
- In the legal world, information is power. By listening carefully, **you gain access to a treasure trove of insights**, not just about the facts of a case but the motivations, fears, and desires of the

individuals involved. These insights can be the key to crafting compelling arguments or negotiating favourable outcomes.

- Legal disputes are, by nature, conflicts. In such situations, the ability to listen actively and mediate effectively can be the difference between protracted battles and swift resolutions. **Allowing parties to feel heard creates an environment where compromise becomes possible.**
- A misinterpreted contract clause or a miscommunicated legal strategy can have costly and dire consequences. Attentive listening helps ensure that **all parties are on the same page**, reducing the risk of costly errors.
- Sometimes, the most potent responses are the ones left unspoken. In negotiations or courtroom settings, **silence can be a powerful tool** to encourage opponents to reveal more or to allow a Judge to ponder your argument. It's a strategic pause that speaks volumes.

Remember that effective listening goes beyond hearing words; it involves observing body language, deciphering unspoken emotions, and recognising the subtext of conversations. As you navigate the complex web of legal discourse, remember that in a world filled with noise, the art of silence can be your most eloquent advocate.

THE POWER OF INQUIRY: UNLOCKING UNDERSTANDING THROUGH QUESTIONS

There exists a superpower in effective communication that often goes underestimated: the art of asking good questions. Lawyers, often thought of as masters of rhetoric, know that sometimes it's not about what you say, but what you ask. Questions are the tools of discovery, the keys to understanding, and the catalysts for meaningful conversations. Here's why:

- Lawyers are, in many ways, seekers of truth. They seek to **uncover facts, motives, and hidden nuances** that can sway the course of a case. Effective questions can unearth critical information that might otherwise remain concealed.
- When you ask thoughtful questions, you **convey genuine interest**. This builds rapport and encourages others to open up and share their perspectives more freely.
- Legal matters can be complex, and misinterpretations can lead to costly mistakes. **Well-phrased questions clarify points of contention**, ensuring everyone is on the same page and reducing the risk of misunderstandings.
- Lawyers often lead conversations, whether in negotiations, mediations, or courtroom proceedings. Through strategic questioning, **you can steer discussions** that favour your client's interests or your case's objectives.
- As an lawyer, part of your role is to **empower your clients to make informed decisions**. Thoughtful questions help clients explore their own thoughts and feelings, ultimately aiding them in making choices that align with their goals.
- **Good questions stimulate critical thinking**, encouraging individuals to evaluate their positions, consider alternatives, and weigh the consequences of their choices. This is particularly valuable in negotiations and dispute resolution.
- Trust is the bedrock of any successful lawyer-client relationship. **Trust deepens when clients feel that you genuinely care about their concerns** and are committed to understanding their perspective, leading to more effective collaboration.

So, what makes a question "good"? It's a combination of factors, including clarity, relevance, and the ability to elicit meaningful responses. In the legal profession, where precision is paramount, honing your questioning skills is not just an asset but a necessity. Whether you're in the courtroom, the boardroom, or the negotiation table, never underestimate the transformative power of inquiry.

NAVIGATING CLIENT COMMUNICATION

Your clients are not just case files; they are the lifeblood of your practice. To build enduring relationships with them, you must approach client communication with the utmost respect and dignity. This is where you wield power to instil trust, convey competence, and assure them that their best interests are at the heart of your endeavours.

Trust, in the eyes of your clients, hinges on three fundamental elements:

1. **Knowledge:** They seek assurance that you are well-versed in your field, a legal expert who can navigate the complexities of their case.
2. **Competence:** Your clients want to see tangible evidence that you have the skills and ability to represent their interests effectively.
3. **Commitment:** Above all, they must know you are wholly dedicated to championing their cause.

These pillars of trust are not built on sharp suits, grandiose speeches or flamboyant displays but through the very fabric of your communication. Patience becomes your ally when dealing with clients; it conveys that their concerns are taken seriously and that their cases are not just another file on your desk.

Imagine a scenario: you've scheduled a crucial meeting with a client, and both parties acknowledge the date. Yet, when the appointed day arrives, you fail to show up, expressing bewilderment when your client reaches out. What message does this convey? Your client may interpret it as forgetfulness or a cavalier attitude towards their case. Trust erodes, and they may contemplate seeking representation elsewhere.

Professionalism in client communication is essential. Maintain a respectful tone and refrain from overly casual or buddy-like interactions. Even if you have a personal relationship with a client, remember that discussions involving legal matters must remain firmly rooted in professionalism.

Expectation management is a vital facet of client communication. Many clients enter the legal arena with misconceptions, believing that hiring a lawyer will magically resolve their issues, especially if they've invested substantially. It's your responsibility to guide them through dispelling these illusions.

Keep the lines of communication open and transparent. **Break down the process (and the legal jargon), outline milestones, and regularly update your clients on progress**. This proactive approach can help avoid situations where anxious clients repeatedly call or make unscheduled visits, seeking clarity. By keeping them informed, you foster trust and mitigate potential misunderstandings.

Client communication is more than just conveying information; it's the foundation for lasting trust. Embrace the responsibility of being a trustworthy advocate and guide, and your clients will seek your counsel and refer others to experience the same professionalism and commitment that define your practice.

NURTURING CLIENT RELATIONS: DEALING WITH CONCERNS AND BOUNDARIES

Adept communication serves as a bridge to address concerns and conflicts, ultimately nurturing robust client relationships. As you embark on your legal journey, brace yourself for the inevitable twists and turns, where meticulous planning often leads to unexpected scheduling clashes or emergent case complications. Instead of sweeping these challenges under the rug, seize the opportunity to confront them head-on.

Clients, being human, may initially react with disappointment when confronted with such issues. However, don't underestimate the power of transparency. You'll reinforce their trust in your professionalism by candidly explaining the problem and your proactive efforts to resolve it.

While fostering strong client relationships is paramount, **it's crucial to maintain the boundary between lawyer and friend**. Your role as a lawyer is to provide legal counsel, not personal therapy or advice. Objectivity should always be your compass.

Drawing a clear line between advice and counselling is imperative. Your clients seek your legal acumen, so your guidance should remain rooted in solving their legal issues, not delving into their personal struggles. Encourage clients who require therapeutic assistance to seek professional help from a therapist, as you lack the expertise to provide the necessary support. While well-intentioned, veering into counselling can complicate matters without delivering the essential assistance.

As you navigate your legal career, you may encounter clients with whom you naturally click. Shared values and interests can pave the way for close associations, but **be cautious not to let this friendship blur the lines of objectivity**.

Maintaining impartiality and objectivity is your ethical duty as a lawyer. Friendships can lead to subjective judgments, making it easy to excuse behaviours that would be scrutinised more closely in other circumstances. This subjective lens can endanger the case and even your legal career.

If you find yourself entering into a friendship with a client, taking a step back is essential. Inform the client that you can no longer represent them and guide them to seek counsel elsewhere. This ensures the sanctity of your professional responsibilities remains intact while preserving the personal relationship.

Clients often turn to lawyers during some of their most stressful moments. These moments can foster a sense of dependence, with clients viewing their lawyers as a vital pillar of support. In such scenarios, **maintaining professional and ethical boundaries is paramount**.

When a client confides in you during times of distress, it's not uncommon for them to develop a sense of dependence. They may come to rely on you for emotional support, viewing you as their confidant. However, it's crucial to remember that your primary role is to provide legal advice, not to become their emotional crutch.

Resist the urge to offer physical comfort, like a comforting touch or a shoulder to lean on (but also remember that you are a human being and so is your client). Moreover, it's essential to **establish boundaries regarding accessibility**. While empathy is essential, it's not your responsibility to offer around-the-clock emotional support. When clients veer off-topic, redirect conversations back to the legal matters at hand, ensuring that your interactions remain professional and focused on legal solutions.

Maintain a level of detachment when dealing with your clients. Avoid oversharing personal issues, even if you encounter exceptionally kind clients. While they may appear sympathetic, remember that your client is not your therapist, and your role is to provide legal counsel, not seek emotional support from them.

Time is a precious commodity in the legal profession, and effective management is critical to avoiding burnout. Some clients may seek advice but hesitate to take action, resulting in prolonged interactions. While it may seem tempting to keep such clients around, billing by the hour, the long-term consequence drains your energy and job satisfaction.

To prevent burnout and maintain job fulfilment, **ensure your clients clearly understand their responsibilities in the legal process**. If specific documents or actions are required, communicate this clearly. Avoid repetitive explanations or prolonged attempts to convince clients to act. Your time should be invested efficiently, delivering value both to your clients and your own well-being.

In the intricate balancing act of client relations and time management, setting and preserving professional boundaries is not a sign of indifference but rather an essential measure to ensure your effectiveness as a legal advocate.

Ethical considerations are the linchpin of trust, holding together the delicate balance between professional conduct and personal relationships. Lawyers must tread carefully, ensuring they never cross precarious ethical boundaries.

It's a slippery slope when lawyers become personally entangled in cases involving friends or acquaintances. Picture this: a friend of a friend is going through a tumultuous divorce, and you find yourself casually discussing the case with your friend. Unbeknownst to you, that information could reach the friend's friend or their estranged partner.

The cardinal rule here is never to share personal or confidential information, even in the cosiest settings. You never know who might inadvertently come across this information, leading to dire consequences. If your clients get wind that you've breached their trust, it's a swift route to losing them or potentially facing professional repercussions.

In the age of information superhighways, the world has shrunk, and the dissemination of information has become almost effortless. Internet sleuths can easily trace the source of leaked information and its subjects. Never assume that what you share with others will remain confined to your inner circle. Keep your communications under lock and key, especially when others can access your devices.

Amid the hustle and bustle of legal proceedings, it is crucial to keep your ultimate goal at the forefront: **providing a solution to your client's problem**. They sought your expertise to resolve their legal issue, and your communication should guide them towards a workable solution.

By adopting this client-centric approach, you facilitate swift and professional assistance and pave the way for a thriving legal career.

However, clients are just one facet of the intricate legal tapestry. Communication within the profession is equally pivotal, shaping the collaborative landscape in which lawyers operate. Let's delve deeper into this crucial aspect.

A GUIDE TO EFFECTIVE COMMUNICATION AMONG LEGAL PROFESSIONALS

Law is a bustling ecosystem teeming with diverse players, each with a crucial role to play. To carve your path to success as a lawyer, you must master the art of communication within this intricate community. The ability to communicate seamlessly with various parties is paramount. These include, but are by no means limited to:

1. **Your legal team:** The comrades who share the battlefield with you, fighting for justice.
2. **Your trusty assistant:** The right hand that helps you juggle the intricacies of legal casework.

3. **The receptionist:** Often the first point of contact, setting the tone for your firm's professionalism.
4. **Your manager:** The guiding hand steering your professional development.
5. **Your boss:** The seasoned mentor and experienced hand that can shape your career.
6. **Fellow lawyers:** Colleagues with whom you exchange ideas, strategies, and sometimes opposing arguments in the courtroom.
7. **Courtroom encounters:** Quick rendezvous with legal peers in the bustling halls of justice.
8. **Expert witnesses:** Professionals called upon for their expertise in bolstering your cases.
9. **The Court ecosystem:** Judges, court registrars, security team and many essential staff who keep the wheels of justice turning.

Your written or spoken words and your interactions with the profession directly correlate to your standing in the legal community.

In this interconnected world, there's always someone, somewhere, silently taking note of your every utterance and action, forming judgments based on what they observe and hear. It's imperative to proceed with caution. Jokes, sarcasm, flirtation, or even well-intentioned humour can sometimes land like a lead balloon. Gift-giving should be discreet, locker-room talk eschewed, gossip avoided, criticism tempered, and complaints handled discreetly. Most importantly, flattery or flirty behaviour should not be employed as a means to an end, as discerning professionals can swiftly see through such tactics, which may inadvertently tarnish your reputation.

Beyond monitoring your interactions with colleagues, exercise caution when discussing your clients. A cardinal rule is to never launch personal attacks on opposing colleagues or allege impropriety due to a difference in legal opinion. As a professional, you must advocate passionately for your client without resorting to personal attacks.

Effective communication ensures the wheels of justice turn smoothly. The better you communicate within this sphere, the more adept you'll be at advocating for your clients and orchestrating cohesive efforts for a common legal goal.

The quickest and surest way to glean a law firm's inner workings is by **harnessing your team's wisdom**. Your comrades, mentors, supervisors, and the unsung heroes of the administrative team collectively constitute a treasure trove of knowledge. They hold the keys to unravelling the legal process, guiding best practices, and imparting the art of crafting various legal documents. To master the intricacies of your law firm's modus operandi, heed their invaluable insights.

As a new lawyer, remember that knowledge knows no bounds. Beyond the hallowed chambers of the legal counsel, **legal assistants, often the unsung heroes of law firms**, possess a wealth of wisdom. Having witnessed lawyers come and go over the years, they've absorbed the nuances of the legal world. Approach them with humility and a thirst for learning; you'll find they're more than willing to help you along your path.

Don't be afraid to pose questions; the wellspring of knowledge you tap into might not always bear the title of 'lawyer,' but their experience can be an invaluable guide to navigating your new terrain. Approach them with a genuine eagerness to learn, and you may be surprised at the depth of insights they're ready to share.

Effective delegation is not merely an option; it's an imperative. **Communication is critical for successful delegation**. Being clear in your expectations is crucial when entrusting tasks to others.

Start by articulating what you need done clearly. Ambiguity can be a breeding ground for misunderstanding and disappointment. Clarity in instructions is essential to avoid confusion.

Set clear expectations regarding project completion and deadlines. Failing to communicate these parameters can lead to a disjointed workflow, potentially compromising the quality of work.

Remember that the administrative team juggles various responsibilities. If your instructions need clarification, they might prioritise other tasks, inadvertently delaying your work. Time is a prized commodity; every moment lost on non-billable tasks can be detrimental.

In moments of self-doubt or haste, it may seem tempting to shoulder tasks yourself instead of waiting for a team member. Yet, it's vital to remind yourself that refusing to delegate can fritter away precious time that could be better spent on billable endeavours.

Your day-to-day will include a web of interconnected tasks and responsibilities. **Coordination is critical to streamlining your legal practice** and maximising efficiency. You'll often orchestrate various groups to expedite the process when working on a client's project. Establish open lines of communication and utilise tools that provide visibility into ongoing tasks. Focusing solely on your piece of the puzzle can lead to losing sight of the bigger picture, potentially resulting in inefficiencies.

Your colleagues are teammates relentlessly pursuing justice. Approach them with courtesy and respect. Irrespective of their job titles, **recognise the collective strength of your team**. The goodwill and camaraderie you foster through respectful interaction can be a potent catalyst for career growth. **Effective communication isn't just a skill; it's a superpower**.

PRACTICAL EXERCISES

Reflective thinking can improve our communication skills. When we reflect on our thoughts and experiences, we can express them more clearly and persuasively to others. Effective communication is a valuable skill in various personal and professional contexts. With that in mind, here are some practical exercises that you can use to reflect on the themes of Chapter 5:

1. **Active Listening Practice:** Choose a legal podcast, courtroom recording, or legal lecture. Listen attentively without interruption. Afterwards, summarise what you've heard, highlighting key points and arguments. Compare your summary to the original content to gauge your listening accuracy. Practising active listening not only improves your understanding of legal concepts but also enhances your ability to engage in meaningful conversations.
2. **Observe Courtroom Proceedings:** Attend courtroom hearings or trials. Observe the communication styles of experienced lawyers, Judges, and witnesses. Pay attention to how legal arguments are presented and how evidence is introduced. Don't just observe; take notes and reflect on your observations to inform your communication strategies.
3. **Public Speaking Courses:** Join a public speaking club or enrol in a public speaking course. Some legal societies offer specific training like a Solicitor Advocate Course. These environments provide opportunities to practice speaking confidently and persuasively. Prepare and deliver legal-themed speeches or presentations. Receive feedback and learn techniques to enhance your speaking skills, including voice modulation, body language, and audience engagement.

Incorporating regular reflection into our learning and decision-making processes can lead to more meaningful and effective outcomes in our personal and professional lives.

CONCLUSION

In this chapter, we have worked our way through the critical importance of communication, including the power of listening and asking the right questions. Maintaining professional communication and relationships with our clients and colleagues ensures that boundaries are maintained and expectations are managed. My key takeaways are these:

- Sometimes the best thing to do is to just stop talking. There can be magic in the strategic silence which can be a powerful tool to encourage clients and opponents to reveal more or to allow a Judge to ponder your argument.
- Asking the right questions allows you to find out the information you need, build rapport, demonstrate your interest, and ensure that you are on the same page.
- There's always someone, somewhere, silently taking note of your every utterance and action, forming judgments based on what they observe and hear. It's imperative to proceed with professionalism and caution, always.

What are your key takeaways? Make a note, get a sticky note, highlight, and keep reflecting on how you can incorporate key themes that resonate with you into your daily life.

Chapter 6:

What's Next: Is the Grass Always Greener?

Stepping into the real world of law is a journey filled with challenges, victories, and, at times, uncertainty. As a new lawyer, you've diligently built your foundation, navigated law firm life, honed your communication skills, and embraced the art of kindness. But what's next? Is there more to your legal career than the path you've initially chosen?

In this chapter, we explore whether the grass is actually greener on the other side. We examine the intricacies of recognising when you're ready for the next step, how to spot opportunities amidst the noise, and the art of respectful transitions between employers. We also tackle the crucial question of whether what you need is a new job or simply a new challenge.

We'll guide you through establishing your professional identity and network and making a lasting impression in the legal profession. Lastly, we'll take a deep dive into the transformative power of mentorship, a relationship that can profoundly shape your career.

As you embark on this chapter, remember that your legal career is dynamic. It's about adapting to change, seizing opportunities, and crafting a path aligning with your aspirations. The grass may be greener on the other side, but sometimes, it's about nurturing the patch you have and making it flourish.

DO YOU NEED A NEW JOB OR A NEW CHALLENGE? HOW DO YOU KNOW?

As you progress in your legal career, you may occasionally find yourself at a crossroads, questioning whether it's time to seek a new job or simply look for fresh challenges within your current role. It's a common dilemma that many lawyers face as they navigate their professional journey. So, how do you know which path is right for you?

Signs You May Need a New Job

If your current position offers **limited room for advancement**, and you're craving a more challenging role with increased responsibilities, it might be time to explore new job opportunities.

An **unhealthy or toxic work environment** can affect your well-being. If you've exhausted efforts to improve your current workplace and it's still negatively impacting your life, move on.

Consider **whether your current job aligns with your long-term personal and career goals**. If your aspirations have evolved, seeking a new job that aligns with your vision may be necessary.

Prolonged periods of stress and burnout can indicate that it's time for a change. If you've tried various strategies to manage stress without success, a new job might provide the fresh start you need.

Signs You Might Be Looking for a New Challenge

If you're still enthusiastic about your current workplace and colleagues but **feel too comfortable and not challenged enough**, it's a strong sign that you need a new challenge rather than a new job.

If you **proactively seek opportunities for growth and development**, you might find that your current role offers more. Engaging with your superiors and expressing your desire for new challenges can open doors within your existing organisation.

If you **generally enjoy your workplace, colleagues, and the culture**, it's worth exploring whether you can find new challenges within the same organisation rather than uprooting your entire career.

Sometimes, the feeling of needing a new job stems from a **lack of work-life balance**. If your employer is open to discussing your workload or schedule adjustments, this could be the solution you're seeking.

Ultimately, the decision to pursue a new job or challenge within your current role hinges on your circumstances and aspirations. Reflect on your goals, evaluate your current situation, and seek advice from mentors or trusted colleagues.

EMBRACE YOUR ROLE IN THE LEGAL WORLD

In the complex and ever-evolving field of law, each new lawyer has the potential to be a linchpin – a pivotal and indispensable element in the larger legal machine. In Seth Godin's book *Linchpin*, he explores the concept of being indispensable, of standing out and making a difference in your profession. As a new lawyer, this concept is especially relevant to your journey in the legal world.

A linchpin is someone who doesn't just fulfil the basic requirements of their role but goes above and beyond. They bring a unique combination of skills, attitude, and creativity to their work, making them indispensable to their team and organisation. As a new lawyer, embracing the role that you have can lead you to success.

Think of the legal profession as a complex machine with many moving parts. Each lawyer, from the most senior partner to the newest associate, plays a vital role in ensuring the machine runs smoothly. Your role as a new lawyer is no less crucial than anyone else's.

One of the core messages from *Linchpin* is that **doing your job well every day is the foundation of becoming indispensable**. In the legal world, this means:

1. **Attention to detail:** Legal work demands meticulous attention to detail. Thoroughness is essential whether you're reviewing documents, researching cases, or preparing briefs.
2. **Professionalism:** Maintaining a high level of professionalism in your interactions with colleagues, clients, and the court

is paramount. Consistently upholding ethical standards and integrity will set you apart.

3. **Continuous learning:** The legal landscape is constantly evolving. Dedicate yourself to lifelong learning and staying updated with the latest developments in your practice area.
4. **Problem solving:** Lawyers are problem solvers. Approach each case or legal issue with a solutions-oriented mindset. Being the person who can find innovative solutions is invaluable.
5. **Effective communication:** Your ability to communicate effectively is vital as a lawyer. Whether conveying complex legal concepts to clients or presenting arguments in court, clear communication is non-negotiable.

Standing Out and Making a Difference

Becoming a linchpin in the legal profession isn't just about being good at your job; it's also about making a difference. Seth Godin argues that linchpins are artists – they bring creativity, empathy, and a unique perspective to their work. As a new lawyer, consider how you can infuse your individuality into your legal practice:

- Look for innovative ways to approach legal challenges. Think creatively about how to achieve the best outcomes for your clients.
- Build strong and lasting relationships with your clients. Show them that you're not just a lawyer but a trusted advisor who genuinely cares about their well-being.
- As you grow in your legal career, consider mentoring junior lawyers. Sharing your knowledge and experience benefits others and solidifies your role within the profession.
- Get involved in your legal community and beyond. Contributing

your legal expertise to community initiatives or pro bono work can be a way to make a meaningful impact.

Your Individual Legal Journey

In "Linchpin," Godin argues that linchpins are not replaceable cogs in a machine but individuals who bring humanity and artistry to their work. As a new lawyer, you can be a linchpin in your firm, your clients' lives, and the broader legal community. **Embrace your role, do your job well every day, and find ways to stand out and make a difference**. In doing so, you'll not only excel in your legal career but also leave a lasting imprint on the legal world.

So how do you do that?
How do you step up and overcome resistance?

Steven Pressfield's book *The War of Art* discusses "acting as if" when it comes to overcoming resistance and pursuing one's creative endeavours. This concept can also be applied to the attitude and mindset of new lawyers as they embark on their legal careers.

For new lawyers, "acting as if" can assist you in stepping into your new role.

Even if you're just starting out and may not feel completely confident in your legal abilities, you can act as if you are. **Confidence is not just a feeling but a posture and behaviour**. Approach your work with assurance and self-belief, which can positively impact your performance and interactions with clients and colleagues.

Act as if you are a seasoned professional from day one. This means demonstrating respect for your clients, colleagues, and the legal profession. It includes punctuality, attention to detail, and adherence to ethical standards. By embodying professionalism early in your career, you'll establish a strong foundation for your legal practice.

Take ownership of your work and responsibilities as if you are the ultimate authority on your cases. This involves being proactive, meeting deadlines, and ensuring you deliver your clients the best possible legal services. Acting as if you are the final decision-maker can drive you to make thoughtful and responsible choices.

Embrace challenges and setbacks as opportunities for growth. **Act as if you are resilient and persistent in the face of adversity**. Legal practice often involves navigating difficult situations and having a tenacious attitude can help you persevere and find creative solutions.

Even as a new lawyer, you can act as if you are a leader in your field. **Take initiative, share insights, and actively contribute** to your legal team or organisation. Leadership is not determined solely by experience; it's also about your willingness to step forward and make a difference.

In essence, "acting as if" for new lawyers means adopting the mindset and behaviours of an accomplished legal professional. While you may be learning and growing in your career, embodying these qualities from the outset can help you build a strong reputation, gain the trust of clients and colleagues, and accelerate your professional development. It's about having the attitude that you are already on the path to becoming the lawyer you aspire to be.

But Without the Ego, of Course

While I encourage you to "act as if" in your legal career, it's crucial to clarify that this doesn't equate to arrogance or an inflated ego. The goal is not to pretend you know everything or to project an air of superiority. Instead, it's about adopting the right mindset and behaviours while remaining humble and open to learning.

Leaving your ego at the door is essential.

Even the most experienced lawyers continue to learn and adapt. When you "act as if" with humility, you **remain receptive to new information, different perspectives, and evolving legal standards**. This openness is vital for professional growth.

Legal practice often involves collaboration with colleagues, clients, and other professionals. An ego-driven attitude can hinder effective teamwork. When you "act as if" with humility, you're more likely to build **positive working relationships and foster a collaborative spirit**.

Upholding ethical standards is a cornerstone of the legal profession. **An unchecked ego can lead to ethical lapses**, such as overpromising or taking undue credit. You maintain trust and credibility by "acting as if" with integrity and ethical awareness.

Clients seek legal assistance because they trust your expertise. However, they also value lawyers who are approachable, empathetic, and attentive to their needs. **Balancing confidence with humility ensures you provide exceptional client service**.

Legal practice can be challenging, and setbacks are inevitable. **An ego-driven mindset may struggle with resilience**, often associating failure with personal inadequacy. In contrast, "acting as if" with humility allows you to bounce back from setbacks and view them as opportunities for improvement.

So, remember to "act as if" with confidence and professionalism, but always with humility. Embrace the journey of growth, acknowledging that the legal profession is a continuous learning experience. By doing so, you'll not only thrive in your legal career but also earn the respect and trust of your peers, mentors, and clients.

NAVIGATING THE TRANSITION: CHANGING JOBS WITH GRACE AND RESPECT

Deciding to move on to a new job and change employers is a significant step in your legal career. It's a transition filled with excitement, opportunities, and new beginnings. However, it's crucial to approach this journey with care, not only to secure the best possible role but also to maintain respectful and professional relationships with your old and new employers. Here are some key considerations to remember as you embark on this transition.

Before you start searching for a new job, **take the time to assess your goals, values, and the type of role you're looking for**. Ensure that the positions you apply for align with your career aspirations.

While you may be excited about your decision to leave your current job, **keeping this information confidential** until the appropriate time is essential. Prematurely sharing your intentions can lead to a tense work environment and potentially harm your professional relationships.

When you resign from your current position, do so **professionally and respectfully**. Schedule a meeting with your supervisor to discuss your departure. Express your gratitude for the opportunities and experiences you've gained during your tenure.

Honour your notice period, which is typically outlined in your employment contract or company policies. This gives your current employer time to find a replacement and ensures a smooth transition. **Be respectful of any direction your current employer gives you about how they prefer to manage the change**.

During your notice period, **assist with the transition process** by sharing knowledge, updating documentation, and providing guidance to colleagues who will assume your responsibilities. Prepare file notes, ensure your files are in order, and any critical dates are recorded and readily available.

Avoid burning bridges even if you're leaving a job due to dissatisfaction. The legal industry is a closely-knit community, and maintaining positive relationships can be invaluable for future opportunities and collaborations.

Do not disclose sensitive or confidential information about your current employer to your new employer. **Maintain the highest ethical standards when handling confidential and proprietary information**, whether client files or the law firm itself.

As you start your new job, **be prepared for a learning curve**. Every workplace has its unique culture, processes, and expectations. Approach your new role with an open mind and a willingness to adapt.

Throughout your transition, **seek feedback from colleagues and supervisors** to ensure you integrate effectively into your new environment. Consider finding a mentor within your new organisation who can provide guidance and support.

Changing jobs is an opportunity for personal and professional growth and should be approached with care and professionalism. By respecting your current and future employers, you can navigate this transition smoothly and leave a lasting positive impression on those you encounter along the way.

CRAFTING YOUR PROFESSIONAL BRAND: MAKING YOUR MARK IN THE LEGAL WORLD

In the legal profession, your reputation and the image you project are pivotal in your career trajectory. The concept of a personal professional brand may sound like a buzzword, but it holds immense significance in how you are perceived by peers, colleagues, clients, and potential employers.

Think of your professional brand as **your unique identity in the legal world**. It encompasses your values, skills, ethics, and how you interact with others. It's the sum of the experiences and qualities that set you apart from your peers.

A strong personal brand **establishes trust and credibility** with clients, colleagues, and employers. It signifies that you're reliable, knowledgeable, and committed to upholding the highest ethical standards in your practice.

Opportunities often come from unexpected places in the legal industry. A robust professional brand can attract job offers, partnership proposals, and collaboration invitations. When your reputation precedes you, doors open more readily.

Networking is a cornerstone of success in law. A well-crafted brand can make your networking efforts more effective. It **sparks curiosity and encourages others to connect with you**, share insights, and collaborate on projects.

Your brand should be consistent across all professional interactions, from your online presence to in-person meetings. Consistency helps reinforce your image and ensure that others know what to expect when working with you.

Your brand **allows you to influence how others perceive you**. Are you the go-to expert in intellectual property law? Or perhaps you're known for your dedication to pro bono work. Your brand shapes these perceptions.

In the digital age, information spreads rapidly. **You never know who observes your actions, reads your blog posts, or follows your social media updates**. Your professional brand is a public entity that can reach a vast audience.

Your professional brand extends beyond the legal field. It can impact your involvement in community initiatives, speaking engagements, and leadership roles. **A strong brand allows you to make a broader positive impact**.

As your career progresses, **your brand should adapt and evolve** accordingly. Embrace continuous learning, stay updated with industry trends, and refine your brand to reflect your growth and expertise.

Ultimately, your professional brand is your legacy in the legal profession. **It's what you leave behind for future generations of lawyers.** A well-crafted brand can inspire others and contribute to the positive development of the legal community.

Remember, your professional brand isn't built overnight. It's a continuous effort that requires introspection, self-awareness, and a commitment to upholding the values and principles that define you as a legal professional. By nurturing your brand, you're not only enhancing your career prospects but also leaving a lasting imprint on the legal landscape.

NETWORK EFFECTIVELY

Networking is not about stockpiling business cards but forging real, meaningful connections. It can be a great gateway to mentors, knowledge, and peer learning.

Attend networking events thoughtfully and **approach them with a clear strategy and purpose**. Define your goals – what kind of connections are you seeking? If the event provides a guest list, scout potential contacts and prepare accordingly. A well-thought-out strategy sets the stage for fruitful interactions.

Networking events are full of connections waiting to be discovered. There's no need to conceal your intentions; everyone's there for the same reason. Be explicit about the connections you're seeking and the value you can bring to the table. For instance, if you meet a lawyer from a different practice area, explore the possibility of mutually referring clients. This seemingly small agreement can blossom into a mutually beneficial relationship. **Authenticity is critical; listen actively, ask questions, and follow up genuinely**.

While networking often centres on what others can do for you, remember the power of reciprocity. Instead of focusing solely on what you can gain, **think about how you can contribute**. You possess unique skills and knowledge even if you're new to the legal profession. Foster a give-and-take relationship that enriches both sides.

It's easy to lose track of the individuals you meet, especially in larger gatherings. To maintain the momentum, reach out promptly. Send a thank-you note or message – it goes a long way. If you've promised to assist in any way, honour your commitment. If you're in the same locale, consider arranging a casual meetup. Cultivate these connections actively; they can be the cornerstone of your legal career's ascent.

Networking isn't just about building a contact list; it's about nurturing a web of relationships that propel your legal journey. When you tend to these connections with care and intention, consider your networking mission a resounding success. These relationships will serve as bridges to elevate your legal career to new heights.

UNLOCK THE POWER OF MENTORSHIP (PART 2)

We've skimmed the surface of mentorship, but let's examine how to form invaluable mentor relationships and extract their full potential.

Mentors are the compasses that can guide your legal career. They've traversed the very path you aspire to walk, and their influence can be monumental. Here's what a mentor can bring to your journey:

- **Positive role models:** They exemplify success, setting a high bar for you to reach.

- **Guidance and support:** Through the ups and downs of your career, they offer a steady hand to guide you.
- **Career development insights:** Seasoned mentors provide wisdom about advancing in the field.
- **Knowledge sharing:** They are treasure troves of experience and wisdom.
- **Networking opportunities:** Your mentor's network becomes your network, opening doors to new horizons.
- **Accountability partner:** Mentors keep you on track, ensuring you meet your career goals.
- **Spotting improvement areas:** They identify areas where you can enhance your skills and efficiency.
- **Skill development:** A mentor helps you hone your skills and become a more effective legal professional.

Think of mentors as your tour guides in the labyrinthine world of the legal profession. Just as a tour guide leads you through a city, highlighting landmarks, sharing stories, and guiding you down the best paths, mentors steer you toward career excellence.

When you embark on your legal journey with a mentor, you're equipped with insider knowledge to explore critical milestones and navigate the smoothest routes. However, remember, the journey is still yours to walk.

Embarking on a mentorship journey can be a game-changer in your legal career, but knowing how to start is critical. Here's your compass to finding, connecting with, and making the most of a mentor:

Mentorship opportunities are scattered across various platforms; you only need to know where to look. Consider these fertile grounds:

- **Legal mentoring groups:** Specialised organisations designed for mentorship connections.
- **Your workplace:** In-house mentors can offer tailored guidance.
- **Networking events:** Opportunities to meet experienced professionals.
- **Social media groups:** Online communities can be treasure troves of mentorship possibilities.
- **Law societies and bar associations:** Local chapters often offer mentorship programs.
- **Legal communities:** Online or in-person communities of legal professionals.

Contact your law society, college or university; they might have resources for budding legal minds. Some lawyers are eager to mentor, so watch for those willing to share their wisdom.

Remember, finding a mentor within your law firm may be more accessible, but don't be discouraged if you don't find one immediately; mentor-mentee compatibility may take time.

If senior lawyers are scarce, consider seeking guidance from younger lawyers who've recently been in your shoes. Age doesn't always correlate with wisdom.

Once you've identified a potential mentor, it's time to **prepare insightful questions**. This isn't just about a Q&A session; it's a chance to tap into your mentor's wealth of experience. Ask about their career journey, recommended books, insightful podcasts, training courses, and professional associations.

However, mentorship isn't a one-way street. Listen actively, ask clarifying questions, and follow up on their advice. By genuinely engaging in their experiences, you'll uncover wisdom to tackle your challenges.

Mentorship without goals is like sailing without a destination. **You must have a clear vision of what you want to achieve**. Consider:

- **Professional goals:** What do you aspire to accomplish in your legal career?
- **Mentorship objectives:** What specific guidance or support do you need?
- **Personal goals:** How does your career align with your personal life?

Your goals serve as a roadmap, helping your mentor understand how best to assist you. For example, if courtroom advocacy is your focus, communicate that to your mentor. Without such clarity, you might receive a wealth of unrelated information.

Setting SMART (Specific, Measurable, Achievable, Relevant, Time-Bound) goals ensures you know when you've reached your destination.

Respect is the cornerstone of a successful mentorship. Here's how to foster a harmonious mentor-mentee relationship:

- Do your research. Knowing your mentor's background sparks meaningful conversations.
- Take the initiative to schedule meetings; mentors appreciate proactive mentees.
- Be respectful of your mentor's time. Think about your session, plan what you want to achieve the questions you want to ask, and be specific about what you guidance you are looking for.
- Compatibility matters. If the mentorship feels uncomfortable or values don't align, seeking another mentor is okay. Your career journey should be authentic.

Your mentor isn't your clone but your guide. You will learn, adapt, and, ultimately, forge your unique path to career advancement.

Mentorship isn't just about following someone else's footsteps; it's about gleaning wisdom, discovering your strengths, and carving your distinctive trail to a thriving legal career.

PRACTICAL EXERCISES

Reflecting on our experiences, both positive and negative, can lead to personal growth and development. We gain insights into our strengths and weaknesses, allowing us to improve ourselves. Additionally, reflection can help us develop emotional intelligence and resilience, enabling us to navigate challenges more effectively. With that in mind, here are some practical exercises that you can use to reflect on the themes of Chapter 6:

1. **LinkedIn Optimisation:** Revamp your LinkedIn profile to showcase your legal expertise, accomplishments, and professional affiliations. Actively engage with legal content, share insights, and connect with legal professionals.
2. **Networking Journal:** Maintain a networking journal to document interactions, key takeaways, and action items from networking events or meetings. Reflect on your progress in expanding your legal network.
3. **Mentor-Mentee Connection:** Seek out a mentor within your field or organisation. Initiate a mentorship relationship focused on career guidance, skill development, and professional growth.

Incorporating regular reflection into our learning and decision-making processes can lead to more meaningful and effective outcomes in our personal and professional lives.

CONCLUSION

In this chapter, we have worked through practical steps to help you consider whether you need a new job or are really after a new challenge. We've highlighted the importance of being the best you can be at your job and making an impact through your personal brand. We have rounded out this chapter with a further deep dive into the importance of mentoring, especially when working out your next legal move. My key takeaways are these:

- Take the time to carefully reflect on whether you need a new job or a new challenge. Future employers may be wary of a history of "job hopping", so ensure your next step is strategic.
- Read Seth Godin's *Linchpin* and work out how you can do your job well every day to embrace your role. Change your perspective and step up.
- Transition to any new role with grace and respect. Manage the process well.

What are your key takeaways? Make a note, get a sticky note, highlight, and keep reflecting on how you can incorporate key themes that resonate with you into your daily life.

Chapter 7:

Learn Every Day

Welcome to a chapter that champions the pursuit of knowledge and celebrates the art of continuous learning. The ability to adapt, grow, and expand your horizons through lifelong learning is not just a valuable trait – it's a necessity.

The legal profession is dynamic, shaped by shifting legislation, evolving case law, and changes in societal norms. What you knew yesterday may not be entirely applicable today. Lifelong learning equips you to stay relevant and ahead of the curve.

Learning must also extend beyond standard legal professional development. While staying current with changing laws and processes is crucial, learning beyond the law assists you in becoming a better lawyer. Diversifying your knowledge base can spark creativity, provide fresh perspectives, and broaden your horizons as a legal professional.

As you dive into this chapter, remember that learning is not a one-time event; it's a lifelong commitment. Timing is everything when it comes to learning. You cannot learn everything at once, nor should you try. Whether you're a law student embarking on your legal journey or a seasoned lawyer with years of experience, the pursuit of knowledge remains a constant. Embrace this journey with enthusiasm, for it will shape your career, enrich your life, and equip you to thrive in the ever-evolving world of law.

THE POWER OF LIFELONG LEARNING

Picture your early law school days, where you devoured textbooks, delved into assignments, and unearthed legal gems. Now, as you embark on your career, the game has shifted, but the rules remain the same – learning is your linchpin.

You were a knowledge sponge in law school, soaking in various subjects and skills. Yet, as a new lawyer, you might find yourself focused on the grind – tasks that seem a world away from courtroom drama. Document reviews, lunch orders, and file transfers become your daily rhythm. Vital, yes, but they alone won't elevate you to the echelons of legal prowess.

Bradley R. Staats's book *Never Stop Learning* offers essential insights into the power of continuous learning. Staats' book underscores that in a rapidly changing world, those who can adapt and learn continuously are the ones who thrive. In law, this holds particularly true. Laws, regulations, and legal precedents constantly evolve, making lifelong learning a non-negotiable skill for lawyers.

Staats introduces the concept of **deliberate practice – purposeful and focused practice with the aim of improvement**. For new lawyers, this means more than routine work; it's about targeted skill development. Identify areas where you want to excel, whether it's trial advocacy, legal research, or negotiation skills. Set clear goals for improvement. Continually assess your performance, seek feedback, and adjust your practice accordingly. Improvement comes from refining your approach.

Embrace the imperative of ongoing learning. Take a bird's eye view of your firm's inner workings; understand the machinery of each team. Identify the skills you need to bolster and the gaps you need to bridge. Stay attuned to the ever-evolving legal landscape – new laws, regulations, and court procedures. Armed with your updated arsenal, you can be the ace your team relies upon when the opportunity arises.

Legal waters are turbulent and ever-changing, and those who navigate them effectively stay ahead. Learning is your life vest. **Keep abreast of legal and professional developments**. Dive deep into best practices, the business of law, and cutting-edge technology. Ride the waves of change and embrace updates in your practice area and court systems.

But remember, while being informed is crucial, it's equally important to strike a balance. Allocate dedicated time for learning amidst your demanding schedule. After all, being "on" constantly leaves little room for meaningful growth.

Opportunity is a rare gem in the competitive arena of law. To unearth it, you must be a keen observer of your surroundings. Learn about national and local happenings, new legislation, and legal issues. This **knowledge is your ticket to growth and advancement**.

As a lawyer, confidence is your armour. It can waver in the presence of seasoned peers or within the hallowed courtrooms. But your secret weapon lies in research, learning, and preparation. The more you know, the surer your stance.

The trick lies in recognising your unique needs and aspirations, crafting a learning journey that fits, and embracing change as your constant companion.

STAYING CURRENT: NAVIGATING PROFESSIONAL DEVELOPMENTS IN A BUSY WORLD

Change is constant. New precedents, legislation, and case law emerge regularly, shaping how legal professionals navigate their practice. Staying current with these professional developments is not just an option; it's an essential commitment to maintaining competence and serving your clients effectively. However, the demanding nature of legal work often raises the question: How do you find the time to stay current, especially when your plate is already overflowing?

The legal landscape is constantly evolving, and Judges, clients, and opposing counsel expect you to be well-versed in the latest developments. **Ignorance of recent changes can not only harm your clients' interests but also erode your professional reputation**.

Finding time for professional development in a bustling legal practice may seem like an impossible challenge. However, time management is crucial, and **dedicating even a small portion of your schedule to learning can yield significant benefits**. Allocate specific slots in your calendar, avoid multitasking, and minimise distractions during your learning time. Prioritise learning as an integral part of your professional life. Recognise that **staying current is not a luxury but a necessity**, and it deserves a place on your daily or weekly agenda.

Setting achievable learning goals is essential. Rather than overwhelming yourself with an extensive reading list or attending every possible seminar, **focus on specific topics or areas that directly impact your practice**. This targeted approach can make your learning efforts more manageable.

Embrace technology to your advantage. Subscribe to legal news websites, podcasts, or newsletters that provide concise updates on recent developments. Make the most of your commuting time or downtime between appointments. Use legal research tools to filter and access the most relevant information efficiently.

Engage with your legal peers and colleagues. Networking events, professional associations, and online forums provide opportunities to discuss and share insights about recent developments. **Collaborative learning can be both enriching and time-efficient**.

Ultimately, staying current should not be viewed as an additional burden but as an essential part of your professional growth. By committing to continuous learning, you enhance your competence and position yourself as a trusted and respected legal professional.

Knowledge is your most powerful tool. Prioritising staying up to date with professional developments is an investment in your career, your clients, and your ability to thrive in the ever-evolving world of law. By incorporating learning into your daily routine, you'll be well-prepared to handle any question, challenge, or opportunity that comes your way, ensuring that you never find yourself unprepared when it matters most.

LEARNING BEYOND THE LAW

The gravity of the law cannot be overstated in the legal profession. It is the foundation of our work, expertise, and ability to advocate for justice. However, there exists a realm beyond the confines of legal texts, courtrooms, and statutes that can significantly enrich your journey as a lawyer.

When you step outside law and immerse yourself in diverse subjects, **you open the door to a world of perspectives** you might never have encountered within the confines of your legal education. Learning about history, sociology, psychology, science, art, or philosophy can reshape how you approach legal issues, helping you see cases, clients, and problems from angles you hadn't considered before.

Legal professionals often work within well-defined frameworks and precedents. Exploring topics beyond the law **invites you to question these established norms and think critically**. You may find that ideas from other disciplines challenge your assumptions, forcing you to reevaluate your perspectives and strategies.

Creativity is not exclusive to artists and innovators. Legal professionals can harness their creativity to find unique solutions and approaches. **Learning about diverse subjects can act as a catalyst for creativity by providing new insights and inspiration**. You might discover that a concept from literature or a principle from science can be applied creatively to your legal work.

Effective communication is a cornerstone of the legal profession. Delving into topics beyond the law can **enhance your ability to communicate with clients, colleagues, and judges**. Drawing on analogies and examples from other domains can make complex legal concepts more accessible and relatable.

The law does not exist in a vacuum; it evolves in response to societal changes. To be an effective legal professional, **it's crucial to understand the broader context in which your work operates**. Learning about social, political, and cultural developments keeps you informed and helps you anticipate legal trends.

The most groundbreaking solutions often arise from interdisciplinary collaboration. Expanding your knowledge into various subjects makes you **a more valuable collaborator within and outside the legal field**. This can lead to innovative approaches and more comprehensive problem-solving.

As you embark on your lifelong learning journey, remember that knowledge knows no bounds. While the law provides the framework for your professional endeavours, the insights gained from exploring topics beyond the law can ignite your imagination, enrich your legal practice, and elevate your contributions to the field. By embracing this multifaceted approach to learning, you'll be better equipped to thrive in the ever-evolving landscape of law and make a lasting impact on those you serve.

BALANCING THE SCALES OF LEARNING: TIMING IS KEY

The decision to pursue further education will inevitably become a relevant consideration as your career progresses. However, like a chess game, the timing of your move is crucial. Before you dive into the world of master's degrees or specialisations, consider the chess pieces already on your board.

Take a moment to survey the daily tasks that fill your legal plate. Are you already juggling a complex array of responsibilities? Ponder the feasibility of adding the weight of further specialisation to your existing load. **Consider how this newfound learning commitment will integrate with your current tasks** and whether your plate can bear the additional knowledge offerings without overflowing.

Time, the most precious currency in the legal profession, is another vital factor. **Can you dedicate sufficient hours to attending classes, studying, and completing assignments** while continuing to discharge your professional duties? Keep in mind that legal practice is fraught with unexpected emergencies. Thus, anticipate the occasional need to rearrange your schedule and ask yourself if you're prepared for such a balancing act.

Reflect on your current state of well-being. Can you manage the dual rigours of work and education without compromising your physical and mental health? Striking the right balance is crucial. **Overextending yourself can render your endeavours counterproductive**, hampering your work and educational progress.

Consider your support network carefully. Will your law firm rally behind your educational pursuit? Does your family understand and endorse your decision, or will it potentially create discord? An unsupportive boss can strain your juggling act, making it challenging to secure the financial support you might need. Family resistance can also hinder your ability to allocate time to your studies.

Finally, **think deeply about your motivations**. In the high-pressure legal environment, it's easy to feel the need to keep pace with your accomplished peers. The allure of better opportunities, pay, and hours through further education may beckon strongly. Yet, scrutinise these motivations objectively. Is now the right time to pursue a master's degree, or would a more opportune moment arise in the future?

Remember, education aims to equip you with the tools and knowledge to excel in your profession. Before enrolling in any course, evaluate the paths it may lead you down. A quality education can open doors to better-paying positions and entail increased work hours and responsibilities. Conversely, passing up learning opportunities could slow your career progression. Weigh the costs against the benefits, lay out your options, and let the scales of your career aspirations tip you towards the right decision.

PRACTICAL EXERCISES

Continuous learning is essential in a rapidly changing world. Reflecting on what we learn fosters a growth mindset, encouraging us to seek new knowledge and adapt to evolving circumstances. It enables us to stay current and relevant in our fields. With that in mind, here are some practical exercises that you can use to reflect on the themes of Chapter 7:

1. **Personal Learning Journal:** Start a learning journal or digital notebook where you record key insights, takeaways, and reflections from your daily learning experiences. This journal can serve as a valuable resource for future reference and self-assessment.
2. **TED Talks Challenge:** Explore the vast library of TED Talks and TED-Ed lessons. Challenge yourself to watch one TED Talk per week that relates to law, communication, leadership, or personal development. Summarise the key takeaways and discuss them with peers.
3. **Book Club or Study Group:** Form a book club or study group with colleagues or friends who share similar interests. Choose a legal book, industry-related publication, or a classic piece of literature to read together. Schedule regular discussions to share your insights and perspectives.

Incorporating regular reflection into our learning and decision-making processes can lead to more meaningful and effective outcomes in our personal and professional lives.

CONCLUSION

Learn every day. We could leave the reflection of the key takeaways from this chapter there. It is more than that, though – we have worked through what you should learn (within and beyond the law) and when you should learn. My key takeaways are these:

- Be a proud lifelong learner. Learn about things that bring you joy, whether that is within the law or beyond the law. If you have a hobby you are passionate about, learn everything thing you can about that hobby.
- Never underestimate the power of learning beyond the law. Embrace opportunities to have your perspective challenged or to think about something differently.
- Timing is everything. When you roll out of law school and into your first lawyer job, getting caught up in the excitement and wanting to undertake more study can be easy. Give yourself time to learn your new role; do that well. You will know when the timing is right.

What are your key takeaways? Make a note, get a sticky note, highlight, and keep reflecting on how you can incorporate key themes that resonate with you into your daily life.

Chapter 8:

BONUS TIP

It's Cool to be Kind: Your Secret Weapon in Life and Law

Let's return to the golden rule from Chapter 2 – "Do unto others as you would have them do unto you". It is a rule that transcends generations and cultures, emphasising the significance of empathy, respect, and goodwill in our interactions with others. This rule becomes more than a simple platitude in the legal profession, where the stakes can be high and pressures unrelenting. It becomes a guiding principle.

Beyond the technicalities of legal codes and case law, outstanding legal professionals are distinguished by their respect and kindness to fellow practitioners, clients, and themselves.

In this chapter, we'll explore the transformative power of kindness. It's not just about being polite; it's about fostering an environment of collaboration, understanding, and trust. Professional courtesy extends beyond our dealings with colleagues and clients. It encompasses how we treat ourselves, acknowledging the importance of self-compassion and well-being in a demanding profession.

In a profession known for its rigorous standards and high expectations, embracing kindness might seem counterintuitive. Yet, we'll discover that it's not just "cool" to be kind; it's essential. Kindness is a cornerstone of effective legal practice that enhances one's professional standing and personal life.

So, as we embark on this exploration of kindness in the legal world, open your heart and mind to its possibilities. Together, we'll uncover how the simplest acts of kindness can elevate your practice, foster meaningful relationships, and create a more fulfilling, compassionate legal community.

KINDNESS WITHIN THE LEGAL PROFESSION

Kindness is a golden thread that can weave together stronger bonds and elevate the entire system. It's a virtue that should extend far beyond client interactions and courtroom dramas, encompassing every individual and role within the legal sphere. In this section, we explore the significance of kindness within the profession, from the support staff to the bench, and how it can profoundly impact your law practice.

Why Kindness Matters

Kindness creates an **atmosphere of collaboration and cooperation** within the legal ecosystem. When lawyers, paralegals, clerks, and administrative staff treat each other with respect and empathy, it leads to smoother workflows, fewer conflicts, and, ultimately, better client outcomes.

Trust is the cornerstone of any successful legal practice. Extending kindness to colleagues, clients, and courtroom personnel lays the foundation for trust, leading to better working relationships, open communication, and enhanced credibility.

Your reputation is influenced by **how you conduct yourself within the profession**. Acts of kindness, such as acknowledging the hard work of support staff or showing courtesy to opposing counsel, contribute positively to your professional image.

So, what can you do?

Take a moment to recognise and appreciate the efforts of support staff, paralegals, and junior associates. **A simple "thank you" or a note of appreciation can go a long way** in boosting morale and fostering a supportive work environment.

Practice active listening when conversing with colleagues. **Show genuine interest** in their perspectives and concerns. Avoid interrupting and, instead, give them the space to express themselves fully.

It's not uncommon for lawyers to find themselves on opposing sides of a case. However, disagreements can be handled with professionalism and respect. **Focus on the issues, not personal attacks**, and strive for a civil exchange of ideas.

Reach out to junior lawyers or law students. **Mentorship is a powerful way to pass on knowledge**, share experiences, and contribute to the growth of future legal professionals.

Be mindful of biases and stereotypes. Actively support diversity and inclusion initiatives within your firm and the legal community. Champion equality and fairness in all your interactions.

Extend your kindness to the broader legal community. **Participate in pro bono work, volunteer for legal aid organisations, or offer your expertise to those in need**. Your contributions can make a significant impact on society.

Kindness may sometimes seem like a rare commodity in legal practice where adversarial roles are common. However, it's precisely in these moments of challenge and contention that acts of kindness can shine the brightest. By embracing kindness in your practice, you elevate your experience and contribute to a more compassionate and harmonious legal profession.

KINDNESS TO CLIENTS: A COMPASSIONATE APPROACH TO LEGAL PRACTICE

It's easy to become absorbed in the complexities of cases, negotiations, and legal procedures. However, amidst the legal intricacies, it's crucial never to lose sight of the human element – your clients. How you make your clients feel during their legal journey can leave an indelible mark and define their perception of your practice.

The Power of Emotional Connection

Clients often remember how their lawyers made them feel more than the intricate legal details of their cases. Whether you're handling a distressing family law matter or a complex corporate merger, demonstrating kindness can profoundly impact your clients' experience. Here's why it matters.

Offering a glass of water, tea, or coffee during a meeting can create a welcoming and comfortable atmosphere. **Clients who feel at ease are more likely to trust you** with their legal concerns and be open about their needs.

Legal matters can be inherently stressful for clients. Your empathetic demeanour, a reassuring word, or a simple gesture like providing a tissue during emotional moments can **significantly reduce their anxiety**.

Kindness fosters a positive lawyer-client relationship. When clients sense your genuine concern for their well-being, it **strengthens the rapport between you**. A strong rapport can lead to better communication and a deeper understanding of their goals.

Clients will remember how you treated them long after their legal issues are resolved. **Positive memories of your kindness can lead to referrals, positive reviews, and a lasting reputation for your practice**.

At its core, legal practice is about solving real-world problems individuals and organisations face. Demonstrating kindness acknowledges the shared humanity between you and your clients, reminding them they're not just cases but people with unique stories and challenges.

So what can you do?

Take the time to **listen to your clients actively**. Let them express their concerns, fears, and hopes. Maintain eye contact, nod in acknowledgment, and avoid interrupting. This demonstrates that you value their perspective.

Avoid legal jargon and explain complex concepts in simple terms. Provide regular updates on the progress of their case and ensure they understand each step of the process.

When clients share their emotions or challenges, **respond with empathy and understanding**. Sometimes, acknowledging their feelings and offering support can be as valuable as legal advice.

Respond promptly to emails and phone calls. Even if you don't have an immediate answer, acknowledging their communication shows respect for their time and concerns.

In court or negotiations, **represent your clients with professionalism and respect for all parties involved**. This will uphold your client's interests and reflect positively on your practice.

Kindness is a powerful tool that can enhance your effectiveness as a lawyer and, more importantly, improve the overall experience for your clients. It reminds you that, beyond the legal documents and courtroom appearances, the heart of your practice lies in the relationships you build and the human connections you foster.

KINDNESS TO OURSELVES: NURTURING WELL-BEING IN A DEMANDING PROFESSION

The pursuit of excellence, the drive to succeed, and the quest for perfection are often seen as admirable traits. However, there's a fine line between ambition and self-criticism, and lawyers need to recognise the importance of kindness toward themselves. In this section, we explore the concept of self-compassion in the legal world and why it's crucial for personal well-being and professional success.

The Unseen Pressures of Legal Practice

Working in law can be incredibly demanding, both intellectually and emotionally. The pressure to deliver flawless results, meet tight deadlines, and manage complex cases can affect mental and physical health. Many lawyers experience high levels of stress, anxiety, and even burnout due to the relentless nature of the profession. Here are some of the challenges that make self-kindness vital:

- Lawyers often set impossibly high standards for themselves, striving for **perfection** in every task. While this commitment to excellence is admirable, it can lead to self-criticism when expectations aren't met.
- Legal matters often involve **high-stakes situations with significant consequences** for clients. The weight of responsibility can create chronic stress and anxiety.
- The demanding workload in law frequently requires **long hours** and intense focus, leaving little time for self-care.
- Lawyers may experience **vicarious trauma** due to exposure to distressing client situations. This secondary trauma can affect mental health if not properly addressed.
- Juggling work, family, and personal life can be **challenging balancing act**, and neglecting self-care is a common consequence.

The Value of Self-Compassion

Practising self-compassion involves treating yourself with the same kindness and understanding that we extend to others. It doesn't mean lowering standards or giving in to complacency. It's about fostering a healthy and supportive relationship with yourself. Here's why it's crucial:

- Self-compassion enhances **resilience** by helping lawyers bounce back from setbacks and challenges. It provides a buffer against the adverse effects of stress and burnout.
- Lawyers often engage in self-criticism when things don't go as planned. Self-compassion allows for a more **balanced perspective** and self-acceptance, even in the face of mistakes.
- Self-kindness is a **critical component of good mental health**. It helps reduce symptoms of anxiety and depression and promotes overall well-being.
- Self-compassion encourages setting boundaries and prioritising self-care, leading to **healthier work-life harmony**.
- When lawyers are kind to themselves, they can maintain **enhanced focus**, creativity, and problem-solving abilities.

So what can you do?

Recognise that perfection is an unrealistic goal. (Ha ha ha lol, yes, I know, but go with it.) While there is absolutely a need for accuracy in all that we do as lawyers, there is a significant difference between accuracy and perfection. Embrace the idea that sometimes work done well is enough and get on with the next thing.

Prioritise self-care activities that rejuvenate you, such as exercise, meditation, reading, or spending time with loved ones. Make the time to reset and "close the stress cycle."

Talk to a professional – a psychologist, counsellor or therapist if you're experiencing high levels of stress, anxiety, or burnout. Recognise the signs that might show you are not coping well. **Ask for help**.

Establish clear boundaries for work, personal life, and downtime. Think about whether you need your emails on your phone and whether checking them when you first wake up is really the best way to start your day. Respect these boundaries as you would respect a client's needs.

Replace self-criticism with self-compassionate self-talk. Treat yourself with the same kindness you would offer a friend facing similar challenges.

Acknowledge your accomplishments, no matter how small. **Celebrate your victories and milestones along the way**.

Kindness to oneself recognises that success is not solely defined by professional achievements but also by personal well-being and fulfilment. By practising self-compassion, lawyers can not only thrive in their careers but also lead healthier, more balanced lives.

THE KINDNESS CHECKLIST: NURTURING A CULTURE OF COMPASSION

In the legal profession's fast-paced and often high-stress environment, kindness might not always be the first thing that comes to mind. Yet, it's a quality that can make a profound difference, not only in your own life but in the lives of those around you and the legal community. This Kindness Checklist will help you cultivate a culture of compassion within and outside your practice. This checklist offers practical guidance on infusing kindness into your professional journey, from your interactions with colleagues and clients to how you treat yourself.

1. **Reflect on intentions:** Regularly pause and reflect on your intentions in legal interactions. Ask yourself if kindness is a guiding principle in your approach.
2. **Active listening:** Practice active listening in client meetings, negotiations, and interactions with colleagues. Give individuals your full attention and show empathy.
3. **Empathy exercises:** Engage in empathy-building exercises,

such as considering different perspectives in legal cases or scenarios. Try to understand the emotions and needs of others.

4. **Random acts of kindness:** Incorporate random acts of kindness into your professional routine. This could be as simple as sending a thoughtful email or offering assistance without expectation.
5. **Mentoring and support:** Offer mentorship or support to junior associates, interns, or law students. Share your knowledge and experiences to help others navigate the legal world.
6. **Conflict resolution:** Approach conflicts focusing on resolving issues rather than escalating disputes. Seek common ground and amicable solutions.
7. **Client-centered approach:** Prioritise the well-being and satisfaction of your clients. Strive to exceed their expectations and build trust through transparent communication.
8. **Positive feedback:** Provide constructive feedback to colleagues and subordinates respectfully and encouragingly. Highlight strengths and suggest improvements.
9. **Kindness in court:** Practice respectful and courteous behaviour in court proceedings, showing kindness to opposing counsel, Judges, and court staff.
10. **Pro bono work:** Dedicate time to pro bono work or volunteering for legal aid organisations to provide legal assistance to those in need.
11. **Community engagement:** Get involved in community initiatives or outreach programs that align with your legal expertise or interests.
12. **Self-care:** Extend kindness to yourself by prioritising self-care and well-being. Recognise the importance of balance and maintaining a healthy work-life equilibrium.

13. **Kindness accountability:** Encourage colleagues and peers to embrace kindness in the legal profession. Discuss the impact of kindness and hold one another accountable.
14. **Continual learning:** Stay informed about initiatives and resources related to kindness and ethics in the legal field. Attend workshops or seminars on compassionate lawyering.
15. **Kindness journal:** Maintain a kindness journal to document your acts of kindness, their impact, and any personal reflections on incorporating kindness into your legal practice.

Remember that legal kindness is not a sign of weakness but a testament to your commitment to fairness, respect, and the well-being of those you serve. As you check off these kindness actions, you'll contribute to a more compassionate and empathetic legal community while experiencing the personal and professional benefits of legal kindness.

CONCLUSION

Be kind. It is a simple yet often overlooked factor in human engagement, especially within the legal profession. Kindness to others and kindness to ourselves are critical in surviving and thriving in legal practice. My key takeaways are these:

- Be kind to everyone (even those who try your patience or are rude in return). Ask, don't assume, and say "please" and "thank you." Watch your tone in correspondence. Don't stoop to the level of others who may not have the same work practices, whether they are your colleagues or your boss. Some days it will be hard.
- Connect with your clients. Show empathy. You are a lawyer, but remember you are also a human being. While maintaining

boundaries is of the utmost importance with clients, connecting and showing that you care and understand their issues goes a long way to building trust.

- Ensure that you have simple daily activities you can immediately do to "close the stress cycle." Go for a walk, meditate, or do a lunchtime yoga session, even if it is just for 15 minutes or so. This simple act is a powerful reset in a relentless profession.

What are your key takeaways? Make a note, get a sticky note, highlight, and keep reflecting on how you can incorporate key themes that resonate with you into your daily life.

Conclusion:

Your Journey to Legal Excellence

Hi there!

Phew! We made it. Thank you for making it all the way to the end of *Thrive: A Guide for New Lawyers* and for joining me on this journey. I used to avoid using the word "journey" – it became overused at one time.

However, the term "journey" aptly captures the passage through a legal career, implying a progression marked by challenges, growth, and discovery, much like navigating the twists and turns of the legal landscape. Just as a journey involves both triumphs and setbacks, so too does a legal career entail moments of success and adversity, shaping one's professional development along the way.

In this book, I have embarked on a mission to equip you with the tools and insights needed to thrive in the dynamic world of law. We've explored the intricacies of mastering time, setting realistic expectations, and nurturing a positive mindset – each a vital component of your professional toolkit.

We have also emphasized the timeless importance of ethics and integrity. Upholding the principles of professional courtesy, treating others with kindness, and maintaining your well-being are not just professional duties – they are the moral compass that guides your journey.

Remember, your journey as a lawyer is not just about achieving success – it's about leaving a legacy of compassion and integrity. With every client you represent, every case you litigate, and every interaction you have, you have the power to make a profound difference.

In a profession as demanding as law, it's essential to remember that asking for help is not a sign of weakness but a display of strength. Your well-being matters, and nurturing it enables you to serve others with greater compassion and efficacy.

At the end of each chapter, I left you with practical exercises and key takeaways. I hope you take the time to work through those and reflect on your own legal practice and the place you hold in the future of our profession.

My overall takeaways are these:

- **Do the right thing, always**. Lawyers hold a unique position in society, entrusted with the responsibility to advocate for justice and the rule of law. This privilege has a corresponding duty to always uphold the highest ethical standards. Don't follow the herd. Don't behave badly because others (even your boss) are doing it.
- **Look after your mind, body and spirit**. Without these, you cannot do your job, or at least you cannot do your job well. Your mind is your biggest asset. Take care of it, nurture it and feed it with knowledge and creativity.
- **Always be kind**, even when all odds are against you and you are dealing with the most obtuse or rude individual. Do not stoop; do not descend into the battle. Rise above it, do your job well and move on to the next task.
- **Stop to celebrate the awesome things you will achieve in your career**, no matter how small (getting through your task list is a daily celebration). Pause, reflect, and lock it into your memory. It will help you on days when things are dark, and you aren't sure why you are doing what you are doing.

Your potential to effect change is boundless. Stay true to yourself, nurture your spirit, and never lose sight of the impact you can make in the world. Your journey is just beginning, and the possibilities are endless. Embrace each challenge as an opportunity for growth, and never forget the power you hold to shape the future of our profession.

May your legal career be nothing short of extraordinary.

Stay curious and keep learning,

Elizabeth

Resources

AUTHOR CONTACT DETAILS

In day to day #lawland, Elizabeth Fairon is a Legal Practice Director at **Life Law Solutions**. For legal assistance in family law or wills and estates planning or administration, you can contact Elizabeth at either her Brisbane or Sunshine Coast office as follows:

P: 07 3343 9522 or 07 5446 1745
Email: mail@lifelaw.com.au
Web: www.lifelaw.com.au

Off to the side of #lawland, you can find Elizabeth at **Acumen Leadership** – a platform offering leadership development, training and mentoring for lawyers.

Email: hello@acumenleadership.com.au
Web: www.acumenleadership.com.au
You will also find Elizabeth on LinkedIn @elizabethfairon

RESOURCES

I've included links to articles. The books you will find at most good book sellers via a quick search on your favourite search engine.

Introduction

American Bar. (2017, December). *New study on lawyers well-being reveals serious concerns for legal professions.* https://www.americanbar.org/news/abanews/publications/youraba/2017/december-2017/secrecy-and-fear-of-stigma-among-the-barriers-to-lawyer-well-bei/

Eaton WW, Anthony JC, Mandel W, Garrison R. *Occupations and the prevalence of major depressive disorder.* J Occup Med. 1990 Nov;32(11):1079-87. doi: 10.1097/00043764-199011000-00006. PMID: 2258762.

Neaverson, G. (2021, March 6). *How are our lawyers? Mental health in the legal industry.* The Lawyer magazine. https://www.thelawyermag.com/au/news/general/how-are-our-lawyers-mental-health-in-the-legal-industry/248491

Walters, M. (2019, April 8). *One in 15 junior lawyers has had suicidal thoughts, research shows.* The law society gazette. https://www.lawgazette.co.uk/news/one-in-15-junior-lawyers-has-had-suicidal-thoughts-research-shows/5069907.article

Leadership: Enhancing the Lessons of Experience by Richard L. Hughes, Robert C. Ginnett, Gordon J. Curphy, 2021

Chapter 1

Eat That Frog by Brian Tracy, 2013

The High Achiever's Guide: Transform Your Success Mindset and Begin the Quest to Fulfillment (Authentic Happiness, Job Fulfillment, Personal Transformation) by Maki Moussavi, 2019

The Art of Possibility: Transforming Professional and Personal Life by Rosamund Stone Zander, Benjamin Zander, 2002

Chapter 2

The Power of Ethics: How to Make Good Choices in a Complicated World by Susan Liautaud,2022

Mindset: The New Psychology of Success by Carol S. Dweck, 2007

Burnout: The Secret to Unlocking the Stress Cycle by Emily Nagoski PhD, Amelia Nagoski DMA, 2020

Chapter 3

The Third Space: Using Life's Little Transitions to find Balance and Happiness by Adam Fraser, 2012

Chapter 4

Just Work: How to Confront Bias, Prejudice and Bullying to Build a Culture of Inclusivity by Kim Scott, 2022

Thanks for the Feedback: The Science and Art of Receiving Feedback Well by Douglas Stone, Sheila Heen, 2015

Chapter 6

Linchpin by Seth Godin, 2011

The War of Art: Break Through the Blocks and Win Your Inner Creative Battles by Steven Pressfield, 2004

Chapter 7

Never Stop Learning: Stay Relevant, Reinvent Yourself, and Thrive by Bradley R. Staats, 2018

Made in United States
Troutdale, OR
11/03/2026

56847401R00100